THE
BED

THE
BED

ALECIA BELDEGREEN

PHOTOGRAPHS BY THIBAULT JEANSON
ADDITIONAL PHOTOGRAPHS BY
LILO RAYMOND

BOOK DESIGN BY JULIO VEGA

STEWART, TABORI & CHANG
NEW YORK

Text copyright © 1991 Alecia Beldegreen
Photographs copyright © 1991 Thibault Jeanson
Additional photography credits appear on page 255 and constitute
an extension of this page.

Grateful acknowledgment is made to Mary Eden Wilson for her kind permission to
reprint from *The Philosophy of the Bed*, Hutchinson, 1961.

Published in 1991 by Stewart, Tabori & Chang, Inc.,
575 Broadway, New York, New York 10012

Library of Congress Cataloging-in-Publication Data

Beldegreen, Alecia.
The bed / Alecia Beldegreen ; photographs by Thibault Jeanson ;
additional photographs by Lilo Raymond.
p. cm.
Includes index.
ISBN 1-55670-180-2
1. Beds—History.   2. Beds—Folklore.   3. Sleeping customs.
4. Interior decoration. I. Title.
GT3000.5.B44B45   1991
392'.36—dc20   91-12827
                                   CIP

Distributed in the U.S. by Workman Publishing,
708 Broadway, New York, New York 10003

Distributed in Canada by Canadian Manda Group,
P.O. Box 920 Station U, Toronto, Ontario M8Z 5P9

Distributed in all other territories by
Little, Brown and Company, International Division,
34 Beacon Street, Boston, Massachusetts 02108

Printed in Japan

10 9 8 7 6 5 4 3 2 1

Page 1: Vermeer's Lacemaker *looms over a bed designed by Philippe Starck for Ian Schrager's Paramount Hotel. Framed in gold, it is used as a headboard in single rooms so that guests never sleep alone. Page 2: The master bedroom of designer Jessica McClintock is in Pacific Heights, California. The walls and windows have been draped in silk taffeta, which is ornamented with rosebud knots. Page 3: A detail of a bed shown on page 112. Pages 4 and 5: This bed belongs to Susan and Tony Victoria of Frederick P. Victoria & Son. Large and sumptuous, the bed welcomes their children as well as the couple. The walls have been covered in chintz, antique textiles cover the headboard, antique and modern linen coverlets cover the bed, and a collection of linen towels and placemats make for unusual pillowcases. Vitrines from the 1930s made from antique wallpaper and fabrics show charming interior scenes of hat shops. Page 7: A detail of a bed shown on pages 100 and 101. Page 10: A miniature bed, made in the eighteenth century by Etienne Nauroy, originally was intended for a cat. It is now included in the collection at the Château Vendeuvre, a museum in Calvados, France, which houses three-hundred small-scale models of furniture.*

To my parents, Joane and Robert,
who gave me love,
the sweetest days of childhood,
and encouraged me
to realize all my dreams.

CONTENTS

THE BED, *my friend, is our whole life. It is there that we are born, it is there that we love, it is there that we die.*

If I had the pen of M. de Crébillon I would write the history of a bed, and what a record of adventures it would be—adventures thrilling and terrible, tender and gay. And what lessons could one not learn from such a record! And what morals could not be drawn for all mankind!

A young woman lies prostrated. From time to time she gasps, and then she groans, while the elders of the family stand round. And then there comes forth from her a little object, mewling like a cat, all shrivelled and lined. It is the beginning of a man!

Then here again are two lovers, flesh pressed to flesh for the first time in this tabernacle of life. They shudder but are transported with joy, and each feels the other's delicious nearness; then slowly their lips meet. They mingle in this divine kiss—this kiss which opens the gate to heaven on earth, this kiss which sings of human delights, promising all, and heralding the ecstasy to come. And their bed heaves as with the swell of the sea, whispers and sways, as if it were itself alive and joyful because it was seeing the consummation of the rapturous mystery of love.

And then again, my friend, think of death. For the bed is also the tomb of vanished hopes, the door that shuts out all, after once being the gateway to the world. What cries, what anguish, what suffering, what appalling despair, what groans of agony, what appeals to joy forever gone, has the bed not known? And what has it not seen of arms outstretched towards the past, of twisted bodies and hideous grins, of upturned eyeballs and contorted lips?

The bed is the symbol of life! The bed, indeed, is man!

From Le Lit *by Guy de Maupassant*
Translated and abridged by Richard Carrington
in The Philosophy of the Bed *by*
Mary Eden and Richard Carrington

MYTHS AND LEGENDS

The bed is a place of mystery. It shares our secrets and knows our truths. It is here that we are born. As our lives unfold and we grow older, our relationship with the bed deepens and evolves. Significant thresholds of experience are crossed here—we encounter the solitude of childhood, embrace the passionate dreams of youth, and mature into the comfortable realities of love and marriage. Our refuge through happiness and pleasure, sickness and pain, the bed accompanies us throughout life, until in death it becomes a metaphor for our final rite of passage.

The bed reflects our social mores and aesthetic sensibilities and expresses some of our deepest human rituals and beliefs. Every culture is steeped in customs, superstitions, and folklore surrounding

17

Page 12: An angel's golden arms gather great sweeps of gold-embroidered muslin that drape from the Empress's bed in Château de Compiègne.

Page 13: Shells, leaves, and whimsical characters are richly sculpted on a late-sixteenth-century bed made of walnut. The bed, from Gabrielle LaRoche in Paris, also has a walnut canopy and sculpted walnut molding.

Pages 14 and 15: The moon and the stars fill a clear winter night sky in southern Nevada.

Page 16: Josephine Bonaparte once occupied this bedroom at Malmaison, a château outside of Paris. The bed, adorned by Jacob-Desmalter's richly sculpted swans and horns, is the one in which Josephine died.

Page 17: "The Death of Sardanapalus," by French Romantic painter Eugène Delacroix, depicts the hedonistic Assyrian king on his bed, watching as his worldly goods and concubines are piled around him in preparation for his funeral pyre.

Right: Hans Christian Andersen's classic fairy tale "The Princess and the Pea" tells the story of a lost princess who proves her royal identity after being unable to sleep upon layers and layers of mattresses and feather beds placed over a small pea. The illustration is by Edmund Dulac.

Opposite: The canopy and curtains that surround the Empress's bed at Château de Compiègne were reconstructed from the original First Empire style. The outer curtains, which are held back by gilded angels, are made of heavy silk muslin. The interior curtains and bed cover are silk chiffon, embroidered with gold thread.

the bed; sleep has been the basis for myth and mystery throughout the ages.

In fairy tales, as in life, the bed is a place of refuge and comfort. While the spells cast upon them may be evil, Sleeping Beauty and Snow White nevertheless sleep peacefully as they wait for a kiss from their true prince. Goldilocks, having wandered off the forest path, finds solace in an unfamiliar bed just her size. And a princess, despite twenty mattresses and twenty feather beds, is unable to sleep through the night due to the uncomfortable presence of a tiny pea.

A bed can be as simple as a mother's robe wrapped around her sleeping infant or a wrangler's blanket and saddle set by the fire under an open sky. It is the place a terrified child will run to, seeking his mother's comforting embrace during the roar of an evening thunderstorm. It has been the writer's study, the artist's studio, the

seat of philosophers' debates. No murder is more heinous than that committed in a bed, no courtship sweeter than that which finds its dénouement between secret sheets.

The bed is also the stage for the most perplexing of all human behavior—the dream. Joseph Campbell, the well-known scholar of mythology, believed that all people, regardless of their historical context, experience similar dreams and mythologies. Some cultures attribute the origin of the dream to the sleeper; others define the dream as a visitation. Without exception, however, the dream is perceived as a path to illumination. For the ancient Egyptian, the word "dream" meant to awaken.

In ancient Egypt, the beds of the pharaohs were richly carved with symbolic animal, flower, and fruit motifs. Fashioned from wood, these beds were ornamented with inlays of gold, ivory, and mother-of-pearl. Headrests carved of wood or ivory were used to support the pharaohs' elaborate hairstyles; foot panels raised their feet. The beds were designed to last, literally, forever. King Tutankhamen (circa 1358 B.C.) took five such beds into his tomb to accompany him in the afterlife. Poor Egyptians, by contrast, by and large slept outdoors, often climbing to the highest available point or hiding under fishing nets to protect themselves from mosquitoes.

The mythologies of ancient Persia and Assyria placed great emphasis on animals as symbols of strength. Consequently, bulls, rams, lions, and large snakes often decorated the beds of Persian and Assyrian kings. The beds were usually inlaid with jewels and placed upon stacks of lush carpets to ensure comfort. By contrast, nomads of the same culture slept on goat skins filled with water—in effect, the first water beds—to insulate themselves from the cold earth.

The Persians were the first culture to employ specific servants to make and arrange their lavish sleeping couches. Beds were considered more desirable if the woven covers and fur-edged blankets were properly made-up. In perhaps the earliest recorded lesson in bed etiquette, the Greek leader Timagoras was given an extravagant bed and coverings and a servant by the Persian ruler Artaxerxes. The servant was included to teach Timagoras the proper way to make the bed.

Beds in ancient Greece were similar to ancient Egyptian beds— they resembled a couch and could be moved easily. They were built of wood and inlaid with gold, silver, ivory, or tortoiseshell. Mat-

tresses, blankets, fleeces, rugs, and skins were piled upon interlacing leather cords. Bed sheets were unusual, but bed covers were elaborate and richly embroidered, as were pillows, which were placed at the head and the foot of the bed.

The ancient Greeks used their beds at banquets, combining both bed and couch for the enjoyment of eating and sleeping. Ordinarily, they consumed four meals a day. In contrast to our tradition of breakfast in bed, their first meal was eaten while standing or sitting and the next three were taken lying down.

The Roman bed was considered to be a symbol of great wealth. The typical Roman bed evolved from the Greek concept but contained several new features—turned legs and the addition of headboards and footboards. A full back provided needed comfort for nights of dining and other pleasures. Mattresses and blankets were made of silk and were richly embroidered. Some Romans slept in a bed with two compartments. They first were rocked in a bed filled with water, then, once asleep, were moved by their dutiful servants to a mattress. Nero, the emperor of Rome, adorned his bed with precious stones believed to have magical powers.

The sophisticated and extravagant bed culture that existed in these early civilizations disappeared with the fall of the Roman Empire. A sack, some straw, and a place to sleep sufficed as a bed. It is from Saxon times that the expression "making a bed" dates—men and women would fill sacks with hay and sleep closely together in hallways for the night. Comfort and warmth were more important than privacy; even the wealthiest families would huddle together near a fire.

In the Middle Ages, a period of great physical vulnerability and psychological insecurity, beds were designed so that the sleeper sat upright, with cushions raising the head. Lamps illuminated the room, swords were well within reach, and beds stood behind guard gates. Thus the sleeper was on guard at all times, prepared for defense. Medieval kings were nomadic, and royal families moved frequently, transporting kingdoms to more fertile grounds. "Bedgoers" packed bed coverings in trunks and moved them to the next royal household, where a full-time watchman would guard the beds' precincts.

By the fourteenth century, canopies and testers assumed great importance. Suspended from the ceiling in the corners of rooms where there was less draft, the draped and embroidered fabrics

Overleaf: Swedish country beds often were built into the walls. These beds, now at Skansen, in Stockholm, originally were in a farmhouse in Halsingland. The linens, cleverly adorned with designs and symbols of the region and piled high on the beds, were embroidered by the women of the house. According to custom, the higher the bed, the more prosperous the farm.

Pages 24 and 25: A sixteenth-century Gothic room was reconstructed inside Castel Gardena in the Tyrolean Alps. The simple Alpine country bed provides a lovely contrast to the ornate majolica stove and painted chest.

21

Above: At Leeds Castle in Kent, England, stands the state bed of Catherine de Valois, queen of Henry V. Framed with oak and equipped with a canopy of equal dimensions, the bed is raised upon a small platform. The silk damasks are woven with symbolic designs: A crown with the royal initials represents the marriage of Catherine and Henry, and a lover's knot represents their hope for peaceful relations between England and France. Beneath the damask bedspread lie straw mattresses topped by a feather bed, fine white sheets, blankets, a bolster, and pillows.

Opposite: This bed, also found in the bedroom of Catherine de Valois, has a style of canopy popular in the fifteenth century. Canopies drew the eyes of the crowd up to the highest point in the room, emphasizing the importance of the person who rested beneath it.

offered privacy and warmth. The length of the canopy revealed the rank of the occupant. Fabric covering the entire bed was reserved for absolute nobility, while a bed that was partially covered was designed for semi-aristocrats. As the Middle Ages progressed, bed designs became more complex and ornate and textiles more extravagant. Beds became so valuable they were considered heirlooms and were often mentioned in wills.

At the other end of the social hierarchy, beds were notably different. The typical person of the Middle Ages cooked, ate, entertained, and slept in the same room. Interiors were spare, with little furniture. Chests were used for storage, as seats, and, come nightfall, as beds. The clothes and fabrics stored inside were used to form a soft mattress. Sleep was a communal affair; it was not unusual for groups of twenty-five family members and acquaintances to share one or two rooms. Many people would share a bed, which is why the beds of that time were often very large.

European history abounds with strange bedfellows, their motives often far removed from the pursuit of pleasure. In the fifteenth cen-

26

tury, an invitation to share a bed was recognized as a mark of political esteem or a symbol of arms laid to rest. The duc d'Orléans effected his reconciliation with Charles VIII by sharing his couch with him. In 1569, the prince de Condé and the duc de Guise bedded down, conqueror and captive together, on the night of the Battle of Moncontour. As recorded in the annals of the Christian church, saints and martyrs, in their perpetual pursuit of chastity, would lie down with young women for purposes of self-mortification.

As a symbol of the pleasures a bed could provide, the Great Bed of Ware was legendary, immortalized by Shakespeare in *Twelfth Night*. The bed, at an inn in Ware, England, originally measured more than eighteen feet wide and twelve feet long and included a large trundle that could be pulled out from underneath. Reputed to have slept anywhere from twelve to twenty people, the bed was often used for orgies. Sixteenth- and seventeenth-century merchants were known to embark on business trips, leaving their wives behind, to enjoy the spectacular seductions of this famous bed.

The bed flourished and found its greatest heights beginning with the Renaissance and continuing through the French Revolution. European culture reached its zenith during this time, and France, the center of European civilization, abounded with the most magnificent beds. Louis XIV, like other French monarchs of this era who indulged themselves in extravagant beds, owned over four hundred beds, many with elaborate ornamented bedsteads and textiles. He was fond of staying in bed, often holding court in the royal bedroom and delivering his mandates from a reclining position. Princes of the realm would be seated close by, chief officers of state would stand, and officials of lesser rank would kneel respectfully.

There are records describing dozens and dozens of different types of French beds used for every facet of living. A partial list includes the *lit en alcôve*, a bed built into a recess of a room; the *lit d'ange* and *lit à la duchesse*, beds with canopies extending from the head of the bed, with side curtains drawn back; the *lit à l'anglaise*, a bed resembling a modern sofa, with a back and two sides; the *lit en baldaquin*, a canopy bed built sideways against a wall; the *lit clos*, a bed enclosed by doors, still found in Brittany; the *lit à colonnes*, a four-poster canopy bed; the *lit à la dauphine*, a canopy bed supported by an iron frame concealed by draperies; the *lit en dôme*, a bed with a dome-shaped canopy; the *lit de glace*, a bed with mirrors at the side

Three wigs on a bed illustrate how common it was for people to sleep together when beds were not plentiful. The bed is in Château Jussy, owned by the Damecourts, in Champagne, France.

Overleaf: The Emperor's bedroom in the Château de Compiègne dates from 1811. The style is First Empire; the furniture is by Jacob-Desmalter.

29

or above; the *lit de justice*, a bed from which a king or other person of authority issued edicts to a formal assembly of subordinates; and the *lit à la polonaise*, a bed similar to the *lit à la dauphine*, but with a headboard and footboard of equal height.

During this time, women were quick to use the bed as a means to establish rank and social influence, and of expressing their fondness for things refined, exquisite, and feminine. Women of nobility were fond of sleeping on black satin sheets (a practice that began in the fourteenth century), which would heighten the highly desirable

Left: The bed in Napoleon's room at Malmaison was made in the First Empire style. The yellow fabric with black ornamental designs is a reproduction. The bed bears a stamp by Jacob-Desmalter.

Opposite: The decor of the King of Rome's bedchamber at Château de Compiègne is largely of the eighteenth century. This room was restored using document silks. The furniture is by Marcion.

33

Right, top: The Venetian ambassador's bed at Knole, in Kent, England, was made for James II in 1687 or 1688. The richly carved and gilded bed with its blue-green Genoa velvet hangings is one of the most sumptuous within the castle. The gilt furniture comprises one of the most remarkable collections of late Stuart furniture in the world.

Right, bottom: This type of trunk was used in the Middle Ages to move bed hangings and coverings from one place to another.

Opposite: Resting side by side at the foot of the ambassador's bed are two gilded ottomans from Knole's collection of Stuart furniture.

The president's bedroom in the Skogaholm Manor House at Skansen, in Stockholm, provides a prime example of baroque interior decoration. The house, which would have been built in the 1680s, has walls covered with early-eighteenth-century "dutch" cloth. The large bed with hangings and the simple clock would have been among the original furnishings of the room. The president and the baroness would have slept in separate wings of the manor house.

whiteness of their skin. Royal mistresses would recline on sumptuous ceremonial beds, *lits de parade,* where they would receive visitors. Expectant mothers of noble blood bore their infants on the appropriately named *lit de travail,* and soon after birth, mother and child would be moved to a *lit de parade* to receive relatives, friends, and attendants. It was customary for the infants to be baptized on ornate *lits de parade.*

The glorification of the bed came to an end with the French Revolution. Beds became a more private and practical matter. English beds in the eighteenth century, for example, were smaller and less architectural than previous styles. Mahogany replaced oak and was a favorite wood of such furniture designers as Chippendale, Sheraton, and Heppelwhite. The first twin beds, designed by Sheraton in the late eighteenth century, originally were created to keep lovers cool during the hot summer months. Sheraton also designed an elliptical bed, an oval shape that would accommodate one person. This elegant bed was a far cry from the Great Bed of Ware, and was a forerunner of the single bed of modern times.

The late eighteenth century also saw the advent of cast-iron bedsteads and cotton mattresses. The two of these made sleeping spaces less attractive to bugs, hitherto an accepted problem. The expression, "sleep tight, don't let the bedbugs bite," has a real basis in fact.

Bed designs in the nineteenth century were often copies of those from earlier historical periods. And the typical contemporary bed, consisting mainly of a mattress and box spring without a headboard or footboard, lacks the impressive architectural elements of some of the earlier beds in history. Our modern culture, however, has given birth to its own legends surrounding the bed—the bed used as a political statement, for instance, as when John Lennon and Yoko Ono conducted their "sleep-in" protest. Winston Churchill is known to have worked from his bed during World War II; Matisse, in his old age, drew on his bedside walls with bits of charcoal attached to a cane. Groucho Marx said "anything that can't be done in bed isn't worth doing at all."

Perhaps the most fitting bed lore comes from some parts of Bavaria. When infants are born, they are placed on a piece of wood that becomes their cradle. As their lives progress, the same piece of wood becomes a part of their bedstead. And after their death it becomes the marker for their grave.

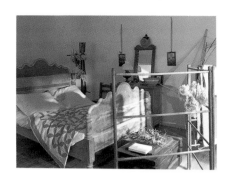

THE BEDS

THE CRADLE AND OTHER BEGINNINGS

he cradle symbolizes the beginning of a new life. It represents the consumation of love and marriage and heralds the extension of a family. Perhaps the most celebrated of all beds, it provides comfort and warmth for a newborn, ensuring safe passage through the infant's most vulnerable stage of life. From the moment of conception a baby rests in the serenity and protection of the mother's womb, and the cradle replicates the primal sensation of rocking and harmonious motion.

The earliest and most primitive cradles were made of hollowed tree trunks. The wood used was selected for its desirable smell (which would have been prominent to the child) and for the legend it represented. Birch, the tree of inception, made a fine bed and was believed to keep the evil spirits away, while elderwood was considered dangerous as it attracted wicked fairies who would pinch the

43

Page 38: A daybed by Mario Villa rests among peaceful greenery in New Orleans. Located on the porch of a Greek Revival house, it is an ideal place for reading or napping on quiet afternoons.

Page 39: A scallop bed constructed of pine belongs to Raymond Waites. A foam and feather mattress was made to fit the unusual size of the bed, and provides soft comfort as well as support.

Pages 40 and 41: Generously draped with silk taffeta, designer Jessica McClintock's master bedroom has a wonderfully airy feeling. At the foot of each bed is an eighteenth-century European folding stool made of iron.

Page 42: The nursery at the Skogaholm Manor House at Skansen, in Stockholm, is filled with furniture typical of the eighteenth century. The curtained bed on the left is from Haga, and the smaller bed, doll's bed, and rocking horse are from Gronso in Upland.

Page 43: A bottle of milk, an antique sterling silver rattle, and diaper pins rest on a mound of soft white linens.

Right: Impressionist painter Berthe Morisot's delicate brushwork conveys the mood of this infant's admirer in The Cradle *from 1873.*

Opposite: Keith Haring created this crib as a token of his affection for his boyfriend, Juan. The piece was very meaningful to Haring, who loved children and was always surrounded by them. "Crib," first seen by the public in a show at Hal Bromm in 1981, symbolizes hope and a new beginning.

Overleaf: A hand-painted toy and hand-knit socks add whimsy to these baby blankets from Pratesi.

baby. As these primitive cradles evolved, they were mounted on low rockers to allow for a gentle movement of the child.

Primitive cultures of New Guinea still make cradles fashioned from twisted cloth, which is slung over the neck of an adult, or from crudely fashioned baskets, much like the one that floated Moses down the Nile. For certain tribes in South America, the human body is the first bed—the infant is held against the mother's skin for the first nine months after birth.

Some cultures, such as ancient Greece, wrapped their newborns in bands of cloth, restricting their movement in the cradle. This "swaddling" held the baby's body and head rigid. Additional security was acheived by passing the bands of cloth or jeweled ribbons that wrapped the infant through holes in the cradle and fastening them to the frame. The custom survived through the Middle Ages and into the late nineteenth century. It was a hazardous practice, as the story

44

Above: Mulford House, an Easthampton farmhouse dating from 1680, has been restored to the way it looked in 1774. This bedroom off the kitchen would have been the warmest in the house, and would have been shared by old and young.

Right: A wooden cradle from Savoye, France, is ornamented with simple carvings.

Opposite: Amid the wares of a kitchen in Burgundy sits a vintage basket converted to a cradle. The mattress is decorated with a cover of white cotton piqué. It is covered with a handmade crocheted woolen blanket.

Overleaf: A bedroom of Lismacloskey House at the Ulster Folk and Transport Museum has two Victorian mahogany bedsteads dating to the late nineteenth century. The long curtains of the half-tester, when drawn, would have cut down on drafts and given its occupants more privacy. The oak cradle is Irish and dates to the late seventeenth century.

of St. Ambrose confirms. He was resting peacefully in his swaddling clothes when he was attacked by bees. The poor saint was completely helpless and was saved only by the wisdom of the bees, who, it is said, recognized the holiness of the baby.

In the Middle Ages, cradles and coverings were often elaborate and costly. Royal infants used two cradles, one for day and the other for night. The cradle used during the day was ceremonial—to display the infant to the viewing public. Elevated, richly carved and upholstered, and draped with furs and precious fabrics, this bed was

48

often as large and as costly as the beds used by the king and queen. Tender and more private moments for the royal infant would take place in the night nursery, where the baby would sleep. The cradle in this room was low and relatively simple. A nurse would sit nearby, rocking the small prince or princess through the night.

Cots and cradles of the eighteenth and nineteenth centuries were elaborately constructed and very often became family heirlooms. In addition to the traditional cradle on a rocker, there was a cradle, or cot, suspended from a post. This allowed for gentle pushing, much like a swing, and reduced the need for constant rocking by hand. The English furniture designer Thomas Sheraton designed the first automated cradle. A clockwork mechanism he invented permitted the cradle to be rocked nonstop.

The nursery of today traces to the Victorian Age, when children were first granted greater recognition as individuals. This is the children's own room, filled exclusively with their toys, their furniture,

Above, left: Using the white cloth straps, a mother would have laced her child into this nineteenth-century Navajo cradleboard. It is from the collection of Iris Barrel Apfel, Palm Beach.

Above, right: Hand-carved horses hold the pole from which this nineteenth-century cradle from India swings. Its platform is made of woven rush, a material suitable for the hot climate. The cradle is from the Iris Barrel Collection at Old World Weavers.

Opposite: Worn strapped to the carrier's back, these Dakota Sioux cradleboards safeguarded an infant by always protecting its head. Traditionally designed, they are hand-beaded on rawhide, mounted on decorated wood, and date from the mid-twentieth century. These pieces are from the collection of Iris Barrel Apfel, Palm Beach.

Above, left: A bentwood cradle demonstrates how practical, everyday objects can also be fanciful works of art.

Above, middle: A fruitwood cradle with spiraling bars has a large voile curtain finished with a double-frill lace border. When the voile is loosened, it covers the bed and protects the baby.

Above, right: Daintily adorned with cotton eyelet and ribbons, this wicker carriage is also used as a cradle.

Left: A rare Venetian cradle of sculpted wood, crafted in a ship motif, dates from the seventeenth century.

Opposite: This wicker cradle sits outside of a thatched house at the Ulster Folk and Transport Museum. The cradle is of woven wicker with pine rockers. A shallow hood protects the baby from drafts. The quilt dates from 1880 and is made of red-and-white cotton with a four-leafed-clover appliqué.

Overleaf: A collection of white baby linens and coverlets, assembled by New York stylist Robyn Glaser, are accented with bows and pastel ribbons.

Right: This French nineteenth-century iron cradle can be wheeled close to a parent's bed. The cradle is very special to Jan Dutton, the owner of a linen company called Paper White; all three of her children slept in it.

Opposite: A giraffe watches over a sleeping baby in this cradle made by Gérard Rigot.

Overleaf: Five children would have slept on this mattress of old straw and wool. Some would sleep head to toe, while others would take turns sleeping on the floor or on chairs placed together. Clothing would often double as pillows and covers. This setting was created by Dennis Severs to show how poor Londoners lived in Spitalfields.

their beds. It is in the nursery that the imagination first takes wing—the floral pattern of the wallpaper suddenly reveals a monkey's face; the breeze through the curtains announces the entrance of Peter Pan; the creak of a floorboard above is a pirate in the attic. Perhaps no better example of these childhood fantasies exists than in *The Nutcracker,* when Clara falls asleep under the Christmas tree and wakes to find her world transformed into every child's dream.

As children move from cradle to crib to a *real* bed, the progression signals new beginnings. Young children become more conscious

Above: A boy's bedroom was converted to a girl's bedroom by draping a small pine bed with lace, bows, and yards of pink dotted fabrics. The small doll's bed has been in the family for over one hundred years.

Right: Mariette Himes Gomez designed this bedroom in her country house. The twin beds were created from her son's old bunk bed; the bedsteads are now lacquered a rich black. Antique Swedish pillow shams, linens by Ralph Lauren, and Shaker quilts dress the beds.

Opposite: Babar, a favorite friend to many generations of children, rests next to a scalloped pillow by Porthault.

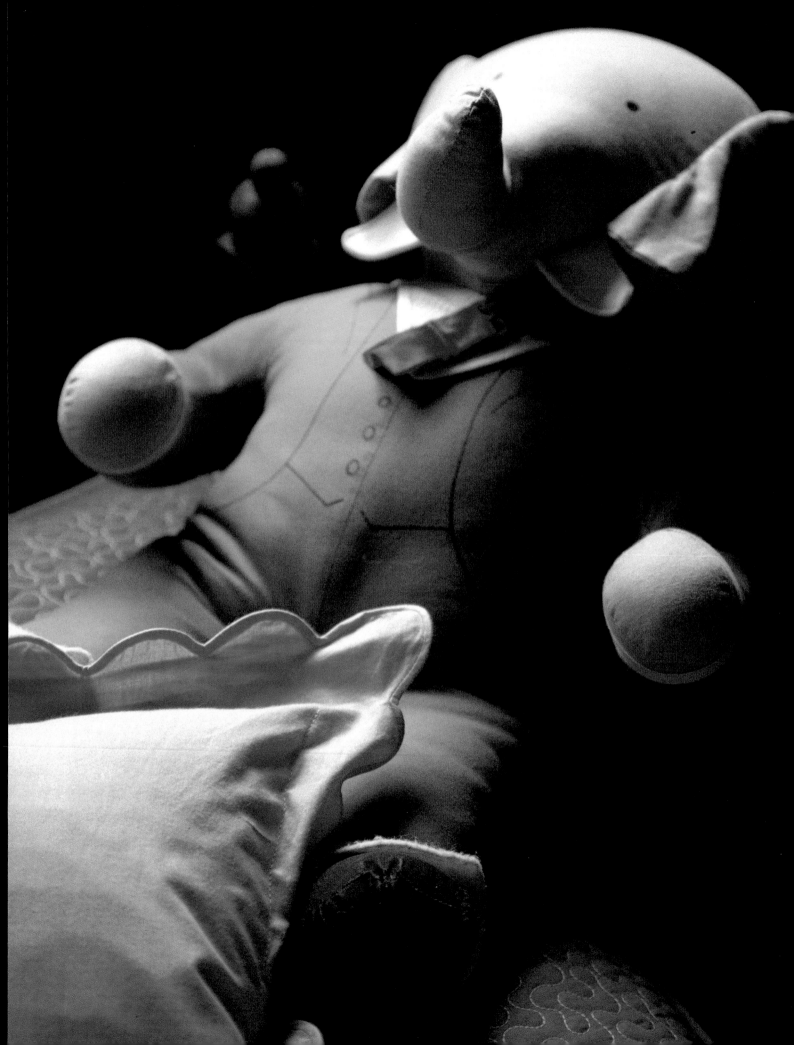

Left: Designers Yves and Michelle Halard keep this bedroom for their visiting grandchildren. The walls and beds have been draped with a Halard print.

Opposite: The Louis XVI doll's bed and small chest of drawers are made of carved lacquered wood. The top cover on the eiderdown is linen lawn, handmade lace, and embroidery. The furniture was crafted by Paquin, a cabinet maker from Dijon.

Overleaf: A boys' camp, designed by New York stylist Howard Christian, uses beds from an army-navy store. Blankets, sheets, and objects personalize each camper's bed.

Pages 68 and 69: Slumber parties are regular occurrences at the home of antique dealers Susan and Tony Victoria, of Frederick P. Victoria & Son. Some children sleep on futons placed on the floor while another sleeps on the daybed. The children enjoy an all-night party while surrounded by beautiful objects: The daybed is a copy of a Louis XVI piece in the Musée des Arts Décoratifs, the obelisk is made of Russian malachite, the mirror behind it is of painted wood and gilt, and the piano dates from the 1930s.

of the comforting ritual of sleep—bedtime stories, fairy tales, goodnight conversations with a parent and a favorite stuffed animal. Their beds become a haven in a sometimes frightening nighttime world; their bedrooms a private playground full of familiar objects and make-believe secrets.

In time, as childhood progresses, independence asserts itself more openly. Children begin to make their own choices about how their bedrooms will look, how they will be arranged—or not, as the case may be. "Sleep-overs" and slumber parties become weekend

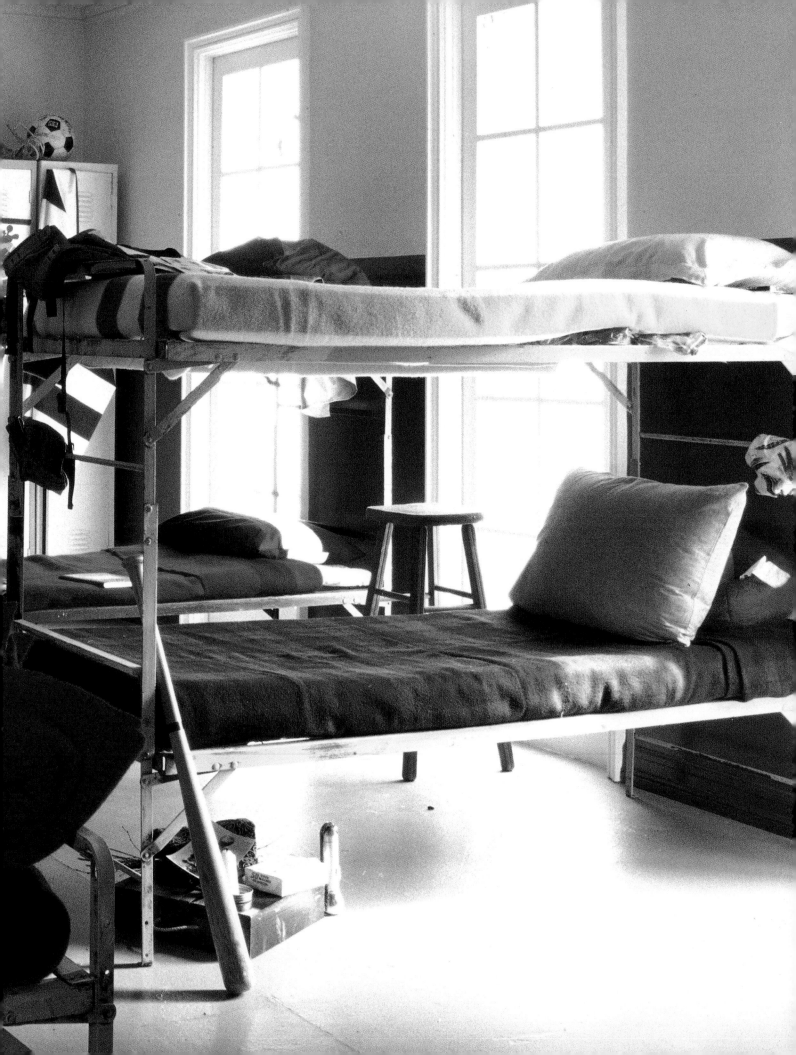

Right: Stashed underneath the striped cotton sheets and Hudson Bay blanket that innocently make up this camp bed is evidence of more adult activities.

Opposite: A detail of the daybed at the Victorias' home shows the transition from child to teenager. The bear waits patiently in bed for the child while a borrowed party dress and high heels offer a more mature fantasy.

events. Bedrooms are filled with sleeping bags and extra mattresses; friends jockey for the best bed or spot on the floor; the unlucky guest is short-sheeted. Camping outside for the night is another rite of passage, as is summer camp. Pup tents are erected, dinner is cooked on a campfire, ghost stories are whispered under the stars. Armed with the sheets, blankets, and pillows from their beds at home, children begin to make their own way in the world.

70

THE BEDS IN-BETWEEN

The "beds in-between" are the beds of transition. They can be as simple as the beds on which we take naps—daybeds, couches, and hammocks, for example. But in a broader sense, they are the first beds for which we are solely responsible. Metaphorically as well as physically, they take us from one place to another, transporting us from one stage of life to the next. Usually beginning at some point during adolescence and continuing into young adulthood and beyond, our lives tend to be in a state of flux. The beds in which we sleep are often far from the homes of our birth and further still from the permanent home of adulthood. Teenagers, students, soldiers, travelers, linked by the transient nature of their passage, all seek refuge in such beds.

During adolescence, the transition towards independence asserts itself in the need to fashion a bed and bedroom of one's own. Mat-

73

Page 72: A hammock hangs in the shade of the Pitot House in New Orleans.

Page 73: Gothic in spirit and construction, this early-sixteenth-century French bed is decorated in an early Renaissance style. Its frame is topped by two mural panels and one column with sculpted diagonal stripes. The decorative panel in the center depicts a mermaid-dragon, the iconographic symbol that casts a good spell on the child.

Right, top: Jacques Louis David's unfinished 1800 portrait of Madame Récamier shows her reclining elegantly on a daybed.

Right, bottom: Beds form orderly rows in French army barracks.

Opposite: This mahogany Directoire sleigh bed was used by Napoleon when he was first consul. It later belonged to Madame Jumel. Ormolu trim and stars give this daybed a dramatic effect.

Overleaf: Don and Lila Madtson of Don J. Madtson Antiques, Austin, Texas, lived in this adobe house in New Mexico. One part of the house dates to the late eighteenth century; the other is from the territorial period. This room remains as their son left it before going away to school. Always welcoming, the 1810 maple four-poster bed, American patchwork quilt, and delightful clutter of toys, antiques, and cherished possessions offer comfort and amusement to every visitor.

tresses are placed on the floor, or the bed is moved, week to week, from corner to corner; posters and magazines plaster the walls, diaries and letters are hidden under the mattress. Teenagers sleep all the time, or not at all, another assertion of their growing independence. And as the struggle for autonomy loosens attachments to the family and encourages the desire to sleep away from home, overnights at friends' houses become routine.

Students, by definition, are constantly in transition. Likewise, student beds and dormitories continue to change dramatically over time. At Eton College in 1441, seventy boys were lodged in a series

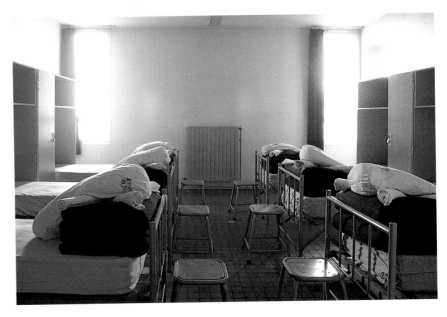

74

Right, top: A bed draped in fabric makes a cozy refuge for a young teenage girl.

Right, bottom: Freddie Victoria designed his room when he was thirteen with architect Russell Riccardi. He lives in a house filled with antiques, and so preferred a modern room. When friends sleep over they roll out a sleeping bag.

of dormitories monitored by three seniors. Boys under the age of fourteen could sleep two to a bed. By 1560, the rule was to rise at 5 A.M., chant prayers while dressing, make the beds, and sweep under them. Bedtime was 8 P.M. These "collegers" were locked in their dorms without supervision and, as might be imagined, maintained a high level of riotous behavior. Bed sports included tossing new boys in blankets and pulling out the bed from beneath a sleeping student.

The modern university student can lodge in a variety of dormitories. Many provide suites where two students in a room share a common bath with two students from an adjoining room. In some colleges, students have private dormitory rooms and share a large communal bath. More recently, many dormitories have become coeducational, thus adding a new element into dormitory life. Whatever the rooming arrangement, the bed is more than just a place to sleep. A simple mattress in a crowded room becomes a beloved and adaptable piece of furniture, used alternatively as a table, a desk, a couch. The bed becomes a temporary home.

Soldiers, if they are able to sleep at all, often do not sleep in

Above: Two elderly brothers who never married live in a nineteenth-century château in Meursault, France. Accustomed to sharing a room since childhood, they continue to sleep in the same bedroom.

79

Above: A Louis XVI bed is now used as a sofa in the Paris home of photographer François Halard and Dominique Velay.

Left: At the Coshkib Hill Farm in the Ulster Folk and Transport Museum an iron double bedstead occupies a room where a traveler may have hung his hat. This type of bed was produced at the turn of the century as a replacement for the older, wooden bedstead. Iron beds were lighter, cheaper, and believed to be more hygienic.

Opposite: A bedroom in this eighteenth-century Swedish house is home for a weary traveler.

Overleaf: A welcome sight after a long trip, the rooms in this Rococo Swedish country house still contain the original wall paintings, furniture, and rugs.

81

Above, top: The first Louis Vuitton bed-trunk was made in 1865 for French explorer Pierre Savorgnan de Brazza. The mattress could be completely folded into the trunk.

Above, bottom: Park benches can function as makeshift beds.

Right: The crew of this Swedish racing boat fits snugly in the built-in sleeping quarters.

Opposite: Made by Orton and Spooner, this Victorian caravan would have been considered the luxury model of traveling homes. The cozy foldaway bed was a welcome niche in such close quarters.

beds. While at war, or training for war, they may find themselves in sleeping bags under the cover of a canvas tent, or huddled against a lean-to, or exposed to the elements in a quickly dug hole. The soldier's formal bed, however, is a study in rules and regulations. A bunk bed in the barracks is made quickly and perfectly—the sheets are tucked in with crisp hospital corners and the blanket is wrapped so tightly around the mattress a coin will bounce off of it.

Beds for travel have existed for centuries. In ancient China strong men carried bedlike structures on large wooden beams; later, horses hauled the sleepers. One of the most unusual traveling beds belonged to Cardinal Richelieu in the 1600s. Bedridden in his old age, but determined to travel, he simply went visiting in his bed. Six

84

Right: A sofa by Mario Villa coupled with an old quilt becomes a temporary bed.

Opposite, top left: Art dealer and fashion photographer Frank Maresca uses this Saporiti lounge from the late 1960s for reading and meditation. The chaise provides a relaxing vantage point from which to contemplate such works as The Jugglers, *by William Hawkins.*

Opposite, top middle: A daybed in the Paris home of interior designer Jacques Grange lends itself to moments of quiet repose and contemplation.

Opposite, top right: Furniture designers Michael Rey and Paul Mathieu were inspired by the curves of Brigitte Bardot lying naked on a feather mattress in Jean-Luc Godard's movie Le Mépris. *Both elegant and sensual, this light wood chaise has a soft feather mattress covered in silk taffeta.*

Opposite, bottom: An eighteenth-century chaise provides a calming retreat in a guest bedroom at the home of designer Jessica McClintock.

men carried the great bed with the cardinal in it, carting it off ships and up hills, into cities and towns, destroying as they went the walls and gates that were too small to receive the bed.

Today, when we travel overnight in trains, airplanes, boats, and automobiles, getting from one place to another while sleeping in bed can take on a special, magical quality. The bed, no matter how simple, seems extraordinary, and sleep becomes an adventure. Pullman sleeping cars were introduced in the 1870s and inspired the ordinary couchette as well as luxury trains like the fabled Orient Express. On

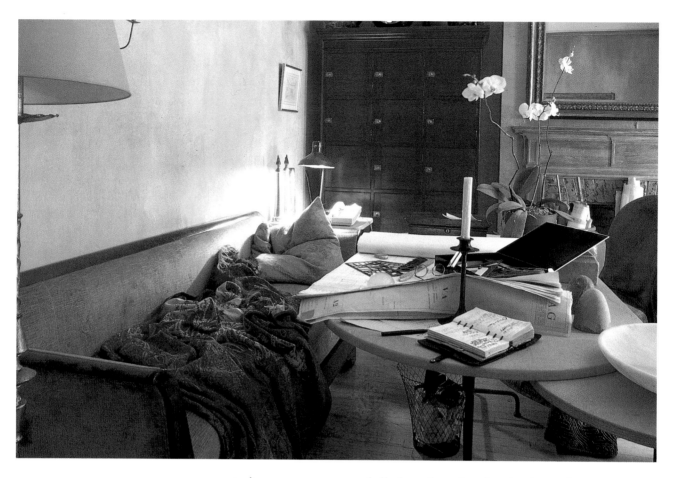

Above: An American Empire rosewood sofa from the 1840s becomes a bed on late nights in the design office of Paul Siskin and Peroucho Valls.

Opposite: During the reign of Louis XVI, the duchesse de Mouchy, lady-in-waiting to Marie Antoinette, occupied this bed by Georges Jacob. French designer Jacques Garcia has draped Veraseta taffeta, dyed to match the color of the original damask, on the bed's gilded frame.

Overleaf: At Skansen, in Stockholm, beds are literally built in between the walls. These beds were piled high with feather mattresses and bolsters, embroidery and lace, slipcovers and hangings. In front of the bed often hung colorful curtains, while at the head was a fine white towel. It was customary for two generations of a family to sleep in these beds. Small niches have been made in the wall to give extra leg room.

trains, passengers are lulled to sleep by the rhythm of movement as the locomotive moves across the landscape.

Airplane beds usually are reserved for heads of state, but such sybarites as Hugh Hefner also have beds on planes. Ordinary air travelers, if lucky, can find comfort on uncrowded flights: a row of unoccupied seats, a blanket, and a pillow or two can make sleeping in the air a restful experience. For astronauts, at zero gravity, sleeping in space requires being strapped into sleeping bags that are stacked like bunks and fastened to the walls. NASA officials describe the sleep as being quite comfortable, with the body floating much as it does in the womb.

Mobile homes, trailers, and a variety of recreational vehicles offer adventurous road travelers a good night's sleep. Beds in these vehicles are well-designed bunk beds, similar to the sleeping alcoves in ships.

Beds in bedrooms, or staterooms, on shipboard can be the most luxurious of all travel beds. Ocean liners and yachts contain beds of all sizes, including queen- and king-size beds. For many people, cruise ships are the epitome of elegant travel, due in no small part to

88

the fine appointments of the stateroom. Smaller ships, like sailboats, can have sleeping alcoves built into their sides. One of the most interesting ship beds is the hammock, which was the standard bed of the United States Navy for over 150 years.

The hammock, originally a primitive bed from New Guinea or South America, is commonly used today for an afternoon siesta. Open to breezes and easy to maintain, hammocks have become standard items for lazy summer afternoons in the garden or backyard. Daybeds are also suitable for napping. They were especially popular in the seventeenth and eighteenth centuries—Louis XIV had forty-eight daybeds, or *lits de repos,* some measuring over seven feet long and up to three feet wide. Daybeds, along with chaise longues, armchairs and ottomans, and sofas, create a special, separate place for naps, reading, meditation, and daydreams.

Above: Dennis Severs recreated the informal boudoir and dressing room of a woman who would have lived in 1825.

Opposite: The Orient Express was inaugurated on October 4, 1883, and was in full swing by the turn of the century. The 1920s and 1930s marked the heyday of this legendary continental train where luminaries slept on silken sheets, sipped vintage champagne, and dined on the finest cuisine Europe had to offer. The train had eleven sleeping cars with both single cabins and double cabins with an upper and lower berth.

Overleaf: Cool Maine breezes on a hot summer day make this simple bed a perfect one for a late-afternoon nap.

93

THE LOVER

The bed can be a place of fantasy or reality. It can be a harbor for trust, safety, passion, and love; it is where physical and emotional boundaries are broken. Throughout the centuries, the bed—whether a blanket of pine needles in the forest or an elaborate bedstead piled high with downy quilts—has been the special province of lovers, the place for lovemaking. Few pleasures are as sweet as entering a bed with a lover—or waking to see a sleeping lover's face. If the lover is gone, the bed seems empty and cold. For Ovid, in the first century B.C., the bed without the lover was a place of isolation and pain.

> What kind of business is this? The bed is hard and the covers
> Will not stay in their place; I thrash and I toss, and I turn
> All the long night through, till my bones are utterly weary.
> What's the matter with me? Am I a victim of love?

97

Page 96: The bed of the lover is one of abandon and mystery. Here candlelight flickers into the early morning while lovers sleep nearby.

Page 97: This four-poster bed on the island of St. Barthélemy is colorfully dressed in striped cotton sheets.

Right: The Bolt, *painted around 1778 by Jean Honoré Fragonard, suggests passion and scandal, not only in the actions of the two lovers, but in the voluminous drapes and folds of the satin-sheeted bed as well.*

Opposite: For hasty lovers, a secret bed of hay is an age-old place to express desire.

Overleaf: This bed was originally a pool table that was found in the rectory at Spitalfields in London. Artist Ricardo Cinalli wanted a high and "proper" bed, so he turned the pool table upside down and rested it on crates from a vegetable market. The bed's frame was draped in fabric, which was then knotted above the headboard. The painted floor and the large canvas leaning against the wall are by the artist.

Pages 102 and 103: Nothing complements a country bed like antique white linens.

Despite the passion and spontaneity of love, each culture has specific rules for courtship—the final goal being to bring the loved one to bed. As early as the fourth century A.D., the writings of the *Kama Sutra* give courting advice to men:

> If your bride-to-be loves magic
> dumbfound her with conjuring and illusions.
> If she's fond of music and the arts,
> charm her with love-songs;
> demonstrate your sensitivity and skills.
>
> On the eighth night of the waning moon
> and at other religious festivals,
> take to her house fragrant flower-crowns,
> a blue lotus to place behind her ear . . .

and

> Persevere . . .
> No matter how fervently
> she loves you, nor how deeply she trusts you,
> you will never get her into bed
> without a great deal of trouble and talk.

Centuries earlier in the West, Ovid was no less stringent in his concern for the proper behavior for women in love:

98

Look, girls: one thing first—you have to think of your conduct. . . .
Necklaces brought from the east, and earrings heavy with jewels. . . .
Nothing is wrong with this, dear girls, if you're trying to please us.

The rules of courtly behavior in twelfth-century Europe were the origin of the expression "to court." In an effort to provide a code of civility for men in that barbaric and violent age, great myths and legends were created to provide role models. *Tristan and Isolde* and the Arthurian legends are medieval manuals of proper behavior. Prior to this era, marriage had been arranged, involving as little emotion as a real-estate transaction. Through song and story, the troubadours created a new cult of personal love. Chivalric courting required courage and manners—and followed a strict adherence to the rules.

In North America of the eighteenth century some courting rituals were truly peculiar. Bundling, the practice of courting the object of one's desire in bed, was quite prevalent. The girl would lie fully clothed next to her suitor. In some instances a wooden plank was placed between the couples. The practice was considered an

Above: Yves and Michelle Halard sleep on the ground floor of their château, Châteaurenaud. The bed, with a canopy of two-tone Halard damask and twill, was originally put together for a fabrics exhibition.

Opposite: A small room large enough for a bed was painted by Marla Weinhoff with gold-leaf falling stars. The full-size Louis XVI bed is upholstered in linen and embellished with a ball fringe. The room was designed by Feldman–Hagan, Howard Christian, and Debra Jason.

104

acceptable preliminary to marriage, allowing courting couples the privacy to share intimacies.

Bundling was practiced up until 1941 in the Orkneys, where a suitor would often travel great distances with little money to see the young woman he was courting. The custom there was to tie a special knot around the girls' ankles.

Modern courtship offers a wide range of options. Men and women are assaulted with advertisements, movies, videotapes, and songs suggesting the variety of ways that men and women can relate. Advertisements—many featuring the bed—suggest that a particular underwear, cosmetic, mouthwash, or car will hypnotize the opposite

Left, top: A sponge-painted finish gives a charming feel to this metal bed in France.

Left, bottom: This bed was found in Raymond Waites's travels through antique shops. He was especially attracted to the bed because of its formal scalloped shape and scrubbed pine finish. A collector of quilts, Waites uses one on the bed and another on the window. More quilts are draped over an antique drying rack.

Opposite: Lillian Williams collects beds and describes them as houses and ball gowns; they are rooms inside of rooms that make one feel secure. This bed in the Louis XVI style is from her collection of eighteenth-century beds.

Above: This twisted-iron bedstead was made by friends of Jan Dutton's in the San Francisco area. Jan, who owns a linen company called Paper White, thinks of her bed as the sweetest place she can be with her husband and three children. In the early morning the family piles into the bed and enjoys watching the light dance through the lace curtains.

Opposite: This sleigh bed, made of bleached wood and topped with a canopy of silk taffeta curtains, is in designer Jessica McClintock's upstairs bedroom. The walls in this bedroom are hand painted.

Overleaf: Hunt Slonem is a painter, bird keeper, and collector of frames. His sense of color is greatly inspired by his many trips to India and Latin America. For him, his bedroom is a place for meditation and contemplation. Pictured here are his family and friends: two toucans, one macaw, and a cat.

sex. The commercialization of courtship is no laughing matter. The often-heard phrase "Sex sells" is true; when people associate a product with successful courtship, they are more likely to buy it.

The irony of courtship lies in the difference between the means and the end. While courtship follows cultural rules, the desired goal—lovemaking—is an exercise of physical and spiritual release that shatters boundaries and restrictions. Indeed, if the rules of courtship are the laws of love, then these laws are meant to be broken.

First love. Young lovers lie awake at night, consumed by the thought of the other. The first lover is torn away from everyday realities and carried to uncharted territories of the heart and mind. Romeo, obsessed with Juliet, declares:

> The brightness of her cheek would shame those stars
> As daylight doth a lamp; her eye in heaven
> Would through the airy region stream so bright
> That birds would sing and think it were not night.

First love is like no other. The bed dances with images of all the

Above: In the Pitot House in New Orleans, a mahogany bed, designed by William Walter and Howard Christian, is crowned with mosquito netting.

lovers we have ever read or dreamed about. The first love bed may be a living-room couch, a hotel bed, the back seat of a car, or a sleeping bag under the open sky. The bed in which we first make love is burnt into the memory like first love itself. As Bette Davis once said, "The sweetness of first love. It still clings like ivy to the stone walls. . . ."

It is at the time of first love that lovers begin to appreciate the double bed. The double bed is a statement of intent, representing warmth, sexuality, possibility. First lovers are quick to abandon the constraints of the single bed for a bed more accommodating of their needs. The double bed provides closeness, but gives space as well to the couple. In sharing this larger space, they allow their love the room to grow.

The first lover is also fascinated by the loved one's own bed. An old German folk tale tells the story of a young suitor, caught in a snowstorm, who gets to spend the night in his love's bed while she sleeps elsewhere. He never consummates the love, but recalls that night as the most erotic and sensual of his life.

When first love turns to passion, the bed becomes the lovers'

112

special haven. If passion is an energy for transcending the bonds of the mundane and mortal, then the bed is surely the vehicle for this flight. Upon the bed the lover finds divinity, eternity, and meaning to life. In Gabriel Garcia Marquez's *One Hundred Years of Solitude*, José Arcadio Buendia enters a woman's bed and is gripped by fear in a classic dilemma; he feels "the bewildered anxiety to flee and at the same time stay forever. . . ."

One would be hard-pressed to find a reference to passion that does not include the bed and some notion of transcending one's own being. William Pattison describes such an encounter in his poem "Nancy the Bed-Maker."

Upon the downy bed displayed,
The unmurmuring, panting, struggling maid.
. . . .
Her slender waist, her taper thighs,
. . . .
Melting, I clasped them close to mine,
And in a moment grew divine!

Above: William Walter and Howard Christian designed this bed, covered with blue-and-white striped sheets, for the Pitot House in New Orleans.

Overleaf: This bedroom and bathroom were created by Ricardo Cinalli and Eric Elstob in an early-eighteenth-century house in Spitalfields, London. A large bathroom was of higher priority than a spacious bedroom, so the space was used accordingly. Built high above the ground, the bed allows for a considerable amount of storage space beneath it. The large frescoes in the room are by Cinalli.

113

Above: Anthea Craigmyle and her family have lived in their house in southwest London for thirty-five years. Five of Lady Craigmyle's six children were born in this George III four-poster bed. Considered the most important room in the house, the bedroom has walls adorned with paintings and drawings of her children done by friends and family.

Right: Odds and ends as well as objects of personal importance always seem to find their way into bedrooms and onto bedside tables.

Opposite: No dollhouse would be complete without its most important room, the bedroom.

Overleaf: This master bedroom, with its bright yellow walls, red silk furnishings, and a paisley carpet and throw, is designed in a mid-nineteenth-century Swedish Empire style.

Madame Bovary is transformed after her first encounter with her lover. Fresh from lovemaking on the forest floor, "She caught sight of herself in the mirror, and was amazed by the way she looked. Never had her eyes been so enormous, so dark, so deep; her whole being was transfigured by some subtle emanation."

Not all lovemaking is directed toward the goal of eternal love. The one-night stand is a brief, intense spasm of passion that temporarily transcends the lover. The bed is often determined by opportunity rather than design; it can be notable or impossible to remember.

The marriage bed is regal. Even the terms describing its dimension bear witness to this status: queen and king. The marriage bed is a commitment to the future and is usually the first purchase of a married couple. It is more than simply a bed for lovemaking; it is the stage for many of life's dramas. Early weekend mornings it can be a playground for children and parents; late evenings it is a parlor for the dialogue of love and marriage. In a good marriage, the bed is full of memories, children, a life together. As the years pass, the bed contains the possibility of death and separation.

Above: A blue-and-white Halard print called "Aurelie" is used generously in a bedroom on the first floor of Châteaurenaud.

Opposite: The luxurious bedroom of Diane de Poitiers at Château d'Anet dazzles visitors with its intricately patterned damask fabrics and embroidery. The superb columned bed is carved with crescents, the mythological symbol of Diana, Roman goddess of the moon and the hunt.

Overleaf: An eighteenth-century iron bed stands in the corner of the book-filled master bedroom of French interior designer, Jacques Grange. The apartment once belonged to Colette.

121

The marriage bed has many interesting customs and rituals. In fifteenth-century England a popular tradition among both royalty and commoners was that of "bedding the bride." In this ceremony, the bride was undressed by her handmaidens and put to bed; the groom undressed by his groomsmen and led to her. The wedding party would then remain in the bedchamber, singing and dancing as the couple made love. Like today's throwing of the bridal bouquet, a stocking would be flung out to the guests to see which would marry next.

The bed of infidelity is the antithesis of the marriage bed. It is a bed of fantasy, belying marriage. This bed is often made with the delusion of love, yet it can provide the individual with the opportunity to reignite lost passions. When Madame Bovary meets her lover, they make love in a boat-shaped mahogany bed surrounded with red silk curtains—a symbol of their transport from their daily lives.

The one certainty of love is that it is ever-changing. For those who journey love's consuming course, the bed remains a constant.

Above: Painter, set designer, and window display artist Geoff Howell says his inspiration comes from a respect for the past. His bedroom reveals the synthesis of his style—one of admiring past periods for their richness in design, color harmonies, and craftsmanship. Surrounding the cozy all-white bed is a comforting collection of antiques, prints, and diverse objects.

Opposite: A detail of Geoff Howell's bedside table shows a charming arrangement of collected artifacts.

Overleaf: Designed by Siskin Valls, an interior design firm, this mattress is made of pullman cloth embroidered in three colors of soutache. The fabrics blend warmly with the room's stucco veneziano walls and stained gold floors.

125

THE GUEST BED

Aguest-bed occupant is a traveler. Whether sleep for the night is sought in a hotel or an inn, or at a friend's or a stranger's house, the bed that awaits the traveler should offer comfort, warmth, and security. In providing a guest bed, the host should offer the traveler a home away from home in an environment that is, by virtue of its novelty, memorable, unique, mysterious, and romantic.

The history of the guest bed can be traced through the centuries. During the Middle Ages, monasteries functioned almost as the sole provider of lodging for travelers. In 1235 a monastery in St. Albans, England, was described as having "many bed chambers, very handsome, with closets and fireplaces for lodging guests." Secular inns, which appeared in the thirteenth century, offered lodgings far less hospitable. Guests slept in a common hall and had to provide their

Page 128: The bed is often the place where one sorts through belongings to be packed away in suitcases and trunks. A tone-on-tone damask from Old World Weavers covers a French Empire bed in the room of Peroucho Valls.

Page 129: A guest room in the Château Ansouis, a tenth-century château located in south-central France, dispels the image of the castle as a dank and drafty dwelling.

Right: An observer of urban life, Henri de Toulouse-Lautrec depicts a moment of intimacy in The Bed, *painted in 1892.*

Opposite: A fresh and lively print called "Les Bouches" adorns this guest bedroom in the Porthaults' house in Emance, France.

Overleaf: The Zorn House, designed by painter Anders Zorn, was built between 1896 and 1910 near Dalarna, Sweden. This guest room was slept in by Prince Eugene, a member of the Royal Swedish family, who stayed here for two to three months at a time. The bed is a Swedish version of a Louis XVI bed. The fabrics are by Mora Hemslöjd.

own food and even candles. In *The Canterbury Tales*, for example, the pilgrims, upon arriving at the Tabard Inn, all shared one room and one candle.

The more modern notion of the guest bed evolved during the nineteenth century, when people traveled in coaches. By 1827, descriptions of inns make them sound quite appealing. One well-to-do lodger left this account of an English inn: "The bed . . . consists of several mattresses . . . large enough to contain two or three people. . . . When the curtains, which hang from the tester supported on substantial mahogany columns, are drawn around you, you find yourself, as it were, in a little cabinet—a room. . . . On your washing-table you find tubs of handsome porcelain, in which you may plunge half your body. . . ." He goes on to recite a litany of appointments— carpets, towels, glass bottles, large mirrors, footbaths, and a "cheerful fire." In less opulent inns, the cost-conscious traveler was generally required to share a room and a bed with several or more fellow travelers. Travelers often brought their own linens and coverings with them.

In Europe it was not unusual for royalty or the wealthy to transport their beds while traveling. King Richard III of England traveled with his own bed and bedstead, and when he died on Bosworth Field in 1485, it was upon his own bed. This practice of traveling with one's bed was brought to the New World by the early settlers

130

who transported their beds across the ocean. Home, in a way, is not merely where the heart is, but also where the bed is.

It is always an honor as well as a pleasure to be a guest in someone's home. It is, however, an even greater honor to be the host of an overnight guest. In order for a guest to feel truly welcome, a host should try to empathize with his or her guests as much as possible: Will they be exhausted from traveling? Will they be comfortable with the sleeping arrangements? Do they have specific personal needs that should be anticipated?

The preparations for a guest's arrival should create a mood in which the guest feels warm and well-received. Sharing one's home can help establish or further an intimate connection with friends and family. A bed that has been prepared especially for a guest—with turned-down sheets, a robe, slippers, chocolates, a night-light, extra blankets, and a good-night note—creates an endearing welcome and sets the tone for an enjoyable visit.

If overnight guests must sleep in a semiprivate environment,

Above: The beds in this New Orleans house are local Catholic convent beds from the turn of the century. Covered in Porthault linens, the beds are at times draped in valances and sheer lace curtains that reach the floor. Mosquito netting, a necessity in this region, probably originally hung from the ironwork.

Opposite: Practical items like a reading lamp and porcelain drinking cup are part of a thoughtful still life on this nineteenth-century American pine table.

135

Above: The Savoy Hotel constructs its beds entirely on the premises, using solid pine frames and natural materials such as horsehair, lamb's wool, and linen ticking. For people who want beds just like those at the hotel, the beds can be special-ordered and shipped all over the world.

Right: Crisp linens and a chocolate mint add the final touch to a custom-made Savoy bed.

Opposite: A suggestive disarray of pillows and duvets cover this bed in a small hotel in Budapest.

Overleaf: This guest room vibrates with the color and texture of pieces from different periods. The room was designed and assembled by Iris Barrel Apfel Interiors of Palm Beach.

136

Right, top: The patterns on the woven covering and linen sheets on this bed at Skansen, in Stockholm, enliven the simply furnished room.

Right, bottom: A daybed at Skansen, in Stockholm, is covered in fine linen and wool. Mid-nineteenth-century provincial Swedish folk art lines the walls.

Opposite: Tucked into an alcove in Jacques Grange's Paris home is a single bed made cozy with a canopy. The curtains complement the green-and-red quilted coverlet.

Overleaf: A carved French pearwood guest bed is the centerpiece of this bedroom that combines sleek and traditional design. The garland wallpaper is by Zoffany. The room is in the Scott Brown and Ralph Jones house, an 1830 late Federal house in Connecticut.

Above: A guest room in this St. Barthélemy villa welcomes visitors with its collection of brightly colored sheets and tropical decor.

Opposite: In a guest room of the Porthaults' house in Emance, France, the head of the bed is made of large cushions hung from a brass bar. A quilted bed cover matches the room's yellow scheme, while a bottle-green pillow with yellow scalloped edges adds a shot of color.

make this clear when the invitation is extended; some guests find sharing a sleeping place unsettling. Every effort should be made to make the sleeping area feel like a special bedroom. A variety of beds—a sofa bed, a futon, a cot, even a sleeping bag—can be made comfortable and inviting in common living areas. A sense of privacy can be provided by using a screen, rearranging furniture, or simply positioning the guest bed away from highly trafficked areas. It is also helpful to establish time schedules so the guest can anticipate interruptions to his or her privacy.

144

Right: The bed is the star of any hotel room according to Philippe Starck, designer of the rooms at the Paramount Hotel in Manhattan. He thought of the room as a kind of artist's studio, so he positioned the bed against a headboard created from a greatly enlarged detail of a painting by Vermeer surrounded by a gold frame.

Opposite: Instead of paintings, the double rooms at the Paramount Hotel have black vinyl headboards encased in gold frames. Guests moving through the room become a part of its composition.

Special considerations should always be given to a guest's bed linens and coverings. They must be fresh and inviting and appropriate to the season—a cool cotton blanket or blanket cover in summer and layers of soft wool blankets or a fluffy down duvet in winter. The luxuriousness of fresh, soft, and smooth bed sheets and coverings under an assortment of plump pillows can transform an ordinary room. A bedside lamp, books, magazines, a carafe of water, and a box of tissues all help to complete the inviting mood. Additional special touches include setting out a new toothbrush, fresh towels, and soap.

Travel can take us to faraway beds in exotic places. The hotel bed can be mysterious and seductive, offering an escape from the routine of daily life. Hotel beds, like guest beds in the homes of friends, can provide the opportunity to sleep with extraordinary bedsteads, sheets, pillows, and quilts. A five-star hotel bed will use the highest

146

quality eiderdown and the crispest, whitest starched sheets imaginable. But a hotel bed does not have to be luxurious and comfortable to be romantic. An old room and a lumpy bed in a foreign city can possess all the magic and allure needed to welcome a stranger.

The hotel bed can be a fantasy bed where one can role-play for the night, week, or weekend. In this rented bed, husband and wife may find renewed vigor in their lovemaking; a new romance may be initiated. The novelty of staying overnight in a hotel bed can be an inspiration.

Left: Crisp linens hang from this mid-seventeenth-century four-poster bed. Baroque Swedish chairs and a vanity mirror painted silver stand elegantly at the foot of the canopy.

Opposite, top and bottom: One of the bedrooms in a Swedish guest house has two beds covered in modern French fabrics that evoke a rustic charm. Gauze draped behind the beds forms small and airy canopies.

Overleaf: Embroidered curtains from the mid-nineteenth century gently frame twin mahogany beds from the same period at Meursault Castle. The beds are dressed in Porthault sheets.

The hotel bed is a different sort of experience for businesspeople. Most regard the hotel bed simply as a place to rest, work, and prepare for the next day. The hotel bed becomes an office desk where work can be spread out and phone calls can be made. But whether the stay in a hotel is for business or pleasure, the desire to receive special care and fine treatment remains the same. When the sheets are turned down at night and a mint or sweet is placed on the pillow, guests enjoy a courtesy that hopes to assure sweet dreams and a good night's sleep.

Right: During a long road trip even the most ordinary motel room is a welcome sight.

Opposite: A trip on the Orient Express can be as elegant and exciting as a stay in a fine hotel.

ON CONVALESCING

The convalescent bed is a bed of transformation. The afflicted enters this bed as if entering a cradle or womb, waiting and hoping to be healed, nourished, and reborn. For the sick, the world is reduced to a bed.

The ancient Greeks believed that healing related to a person's physical body, soul or psyche, and spirit. Healing centers were popular in ancient Greece. A common remedy for many sicknesses entailed seeing a play and going to bed. The bed, sleep, and dreams were thought to have special recuperative powers.

Healing today must still take place in the patient's body, psyche, and spirit. And the environment in which the patient is making his or her recovery is all-important. It should allow the patient to experience a sense of independence, if possible, while providing comfort and visual beauty. The objects that surround the convalescent's bed

155

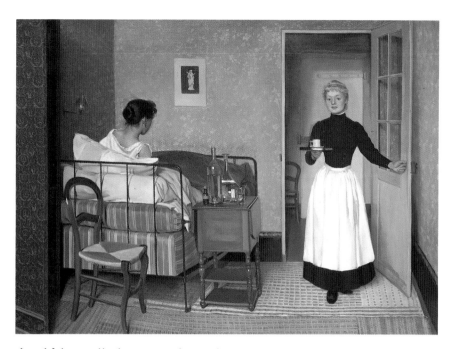

Page 154: All-purpose in nature, the hospital bed becomes a patient's temporary home.

Page 155: Always a thoughtful and welcome gift, flowers add freshness and cheer to any room.

Right: A leader of the Parisian avant-garde in the late nineteenth century, Félix Vallotton captured a detail of real life in The Sick Woman *(1892).*

Opposite: Tea can be a comforting tonic for the convalescent. This Coalport tea set is in Glin Castle in County Limerick, Ireland.

Overleaf: The Great Hall of the Needy forms the heart of the Hospice de Beaune in France, where nuns cared for the sick in the fifteenth century. Two patients would have been assigned to a bed, as opposed to three or four in other hospitals. A curtain could be drawn between each bed for privacy and warmth. The beds faced the altar at the end of the room so mass could be celebrated.

should be well chosen and carefully arranged. Colorful fabrics and fresh linens are small details that can enliven a patient's spirit. Fresh flowers also add color and beauty to the sick room. A glass, a carafe of water, and a pencil and paper belong next to the bed, as does a bell with which to ring for assistance. Heat, proper ventilation, and peace and quiet are important to the convalescent, as are books, a good light, a telephone, and a television within reach. Some patients may also benefit from a worktable near their bed.

The convalescent bed should provide the patient with physical support and emotional security. High rails on hospital beds allow patients to feel safely contained in their beds and prevent any danger from falling. Support mattresses, or a piece of plywood under the mattress, can provide added firmness, if needed. For someone who is bedridden, the bed is his or her universe, and great care should be taken to keep this bed neat, fresh, and pleasant.

Natural fibers are the best choices for bedclothes, since these fibers naturally breathe and absorb perspiration. The texture of the bed linens should be soft and gentle to the touch; the colors calm and soothing, even for young children. When the bed linens are being changed, the patient should rest comfortably in a chair, bundled up in blankets and/or a duvet for warmth. The fresh bed linens should be warm when they go on the bed—they can be placed on a radiator beforehand, for example. After the sheets are changed, change the pillowcases, plump up the pillows, and rearrange them.

156

When rearranging blankets and duvets, allow enough room for the patient's feet and legs to move freely.

The convalescent bed is best placed in a bedroom where sunlight does not enter the room directly, tiring the patient's eyes. If possible, the bed should be positioned with three sides reasonably exposed, providing access for the people who are caring for the patient. A bedside table or cabinet should be placed within the patient's reach; it should remain uncluttered so that objects do not have to be cleared at every mealtime or treatment.

If a patient must stay in a hospital rather than at home, such attention to detail can be even more important. The key to making a hospital stay more comforting is by personalizing as much of the patient's space as possible. Pillows and quilts from home add familiarity as well as comfort, while flowers, posters, photographs, books, and toys add warmth and amusement to empty spaces and walls.

The hospital bed need not be, as Anthony Burgess described it

Above, left: An elderly cousin now occupies the late Mrs. Hope Nicholson's lapis-lazuli and gold apartment. Religious paintings and crosses surround the bed.

Above, right: Holy water from Lourdes is believed by some Catholics to possess healing properties. People continue to make pilgrimages to the small town in the French Pyrenees in order to acquire some of the blessed liquid.

Opposite: A mansion built in 1882 for portrait painter John Collier has belonged to the Hope family since 1892. The late Mrs. Hope Nicholson's lapis-lazuli and gold apartment was inspired by a plate in Leloire's biography of Cardinal Richelieu. Several generations of her family were born in this bed.

161

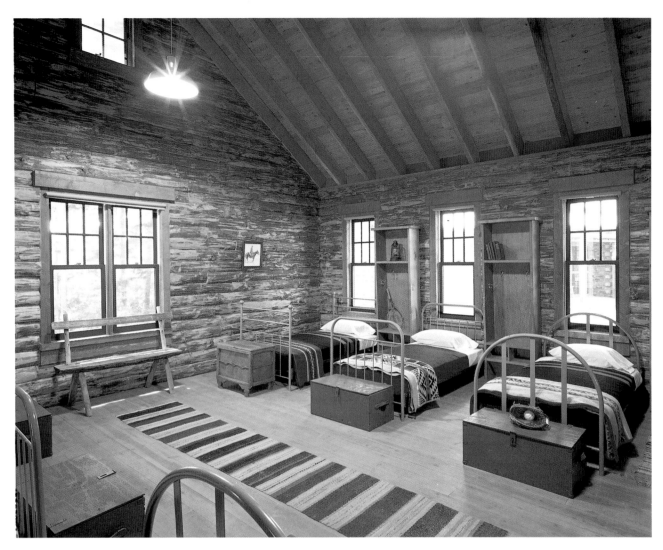

Above: The Hole in the Wall Gang Camp, owned by Paul Newman, is attended by children suffering from cancer or blood disorders. The camp beds have a "Wild West" feeling, as the environment is intended to be as dissimilar to a hospital as possible. Each bed frame is different from the one next to it, and each bed is covered with a handwoven woolen blanket.

Right: The design of this hospital room at Nordform in Moira, Sweden, is based on the philosophies of Rudolph Steiner; color, space, and texture have been chosen for their healing properties.

Opposite: Comfort and convenience are of primary importance to hospital patients. Modern technology has enabled beds to be adjusted to a variety of positions.

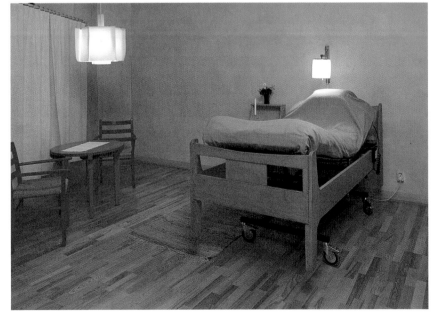

162

Mölnlycke
Mobility

Pages 164 and 165: This room in the house of Mario Villa has been designed so that it does not reveal a particular time or place; although it is vaguely reminiscent of sixteenth-, seventeenth-, and eighteenth-century European styles, this bedroom could have existed almost anywhere at any time. Two French daybeds, or lits de repos, *are made of carved wood and date to the late eighteenth and early nineteenth centuries. The effect of the room is quiet and calming.*

Pages 166 and 167: In Mario Villa's bedroom are early-nineteenth-century santos from North America. Made of real hair and wearing clothing that honors the birth of Christ, the santos are powerful, mystical, and peaceful objects. Villa says he feels protected in their presence as he sleeps.

Right: Freud's original psychoanalytic couch now sits in the Freud Museum in Hampstead, London.

Opposite: When slumber is interrupted by fever, anxiety, or insomnia, the bed duly shows the struggle of a night's sleep.

in *On Going to Bed*, "a machine to accommodate an impersonal, sick organism." Hospital beds can be sympathetic structures designed to make the patient more comfortable. Some hospital beds can be piloted like an airplane by using switches and controls that raise and lower the head and feet. A more elaborate hospital bed can, at the push of a button, make a washbasin swing before the patient, open or shut the windows, and summon a nurse. When Howard Hughes was incapacitated after an airplane accident, he allegedly could move around the room in his bed by using buttons.

Whether a patient is confined to a bed at home or in a hospital, it is most helpful and healthful to keep the convalescent's mind active and productive. There have been many artists who continued to create while they were bedridden. Matisse used to sit in bed painting and sculpting. Rossini composed many of his operas and Colette wrote many of her novels from bed. John Milton composed "Paradise Lost" in bed, the lines transcribed by his daughters. And Marcel Proust, the most famous of all artists exhausted and inspired by illness, wrote his literary masterpiece, *Remembrance of Things Past*, from the confines of his bed.

168

DIFFERENT BEDS

Beds are as unique as their occupants, reflecting how and where a person wants to sleep. The type of bed one sleeps in is usually limited only by the boundaries of culture and imagination. In Japan, for instance, the futon is the bed of choice, while in the United States the selection is likely to be a simple mattress and box spring. Yet within every culture are artists and free spirits who loosen the reins of tradition and let their imaginations run free.

Different beds are unusual beds. The different bed can be a simple flight of fancy or the esoteric realization of a dream or fantasy. It can be a recreation or reinterpretation of a bed from a historical or cultural period. Or a glimpse at the future needs of twenty-first-century sleepers.

What is standard in one culture can be unusual in another. In

Page 170: The bed can be a complete fantasy, as is this bed of straw and linen created in Sicily.

Page 171: Pets also appreciate the comfort, warmth, and protection offered by a bed, especially one as stylish as this.

Right: The "Maharajah's Bed" was made by Christofle in 1882. On every corner stood a large painted-bronze nude, each representing one of the Rajah's ideal women. The women held goose-plume or horsetail fans—those at the foot of the bed to chase away flies, and those at the head to fan the Rajah. The bed was embellished with silver.

Opposite: Like a stage, curtains can be drawn along the length of this metal bed while the headboard and footboard remain open. Designed by Massimo Morozzi for Driade, the bed is supported by red cylindrical legs made of wood.

Overleaf: Armed with cardboard and a can of paint, painter, set designer, and window display artist Geoff Howell created an eighteenth-century fantasy. Silk draperies, hand-embroidered linens, parquet floors, gilded frames, a marble fireplace, and a burning candelabrum come to life in a simple black-and-white rendering.

Japan, for example, most people sleep between two simple quilts: the *shiki* (futon underquilt) and the *kake* (futon overquilt). By day the quilts are kept in a closet, and at night they are unrolled on a mat called a *tatami*, which covers the whole floor of the room. It is considered a major failing in discipline for a wife to leave the futon out after waking.

In India, beds vary from mats to Western-style beds. One type of Indian bedstead is the *charpoy*, which consists of a simple framework of wood supporting a lattice of interwoven ropes. Extremely comfortable, the *charpoy* is sufficiently portable to be moved into a courtyard at night so the sleeper can enjoy the cool air. Also found in India is the "bed of nails," a board covered with rows of upward-pointing nails. Reserved for itinerant Hindu ascetics and mystics known as fakirs, these beds would display to onlookers the fakir's powers to endure pain. In 1969 the fakir Silki claimed to have spent 111 days on a bed of nails in São Paulo, Brazil.

Unusual beds have been created throughout history. An ancient Japanese bedframe, belonging to the royal family, was made from elaborately carved teak and was completely round. Four dragon-shaped feet held it upright. Charlemagne had a bronze tubular bedstead that forced him to sleep at a forty-five-degree angle; this defensive sleeping position was common throughout the Middle Ages. Ludwig II of Bavaria had a bed shaped like a cathedral. In England around the turn of the century, there was a bed, known as

172

Above: Kamp Kill Kare, often considered the grandest of the Adirondack lodges in northern New York State, features this tree bed made in 1916 from an entire tree stripped of its bark. The cottage may have been constructed around the famous tree bed, which reaches to the roof.

the Celestial Bed, said to have magical powers. Those who slept upon its mattress made of flowers and herbs believed the bed increased their sexual vigor and desirability. The famous Christofle bed, a monumental bed made of solid silver, was built for an Indian prince in 1882. At each of its corners was a life-size painted statue of a naked woman, facing the sleeper and holding a fan. Complete with enamel eyes and wigs of real hair, the statues were truly fantastic. When the maharajah lay down, his weight would start a music box

176

in the mattress and the statues would wave their fans. The bed weighed over a ton.

Press beds, beds that are concealed within walls or within another piece of furniture, became popular among the middle classes around the turn of the century. Press beds had a dual purpose, folding into a usable table, bench, chest, or even a piano when not needed. A modern-day example is the Murphy bed, which folds into the wall to allow the sleeping space to be used for other purposes. The concept of the press bed can be found in many cultures throughout history. A traveler in Holland wrote of a bed that was like a cupboard, built into the wall of the room and lined with earthenware tiles. Similar sleeping niches were found in the walls in the ruins at Pompeii.

Many unusual beds are built to specifications, based on a cus-

Above, left: Two sleep "restraints" are included in a model of a typical space shuttle at the Johnson Space Center in Houston, Texas. In space, astronauts need to be restrained while they sleep because their outside atmosphere has no gravity—hence, they are totally weightless. Whether they sleep in a horizontal or vertical position does not matter; with no gravity, people can even sleep upside down.

Above, right: Robert Rauschenburg mounted a quilt, sheet, and pillow on wooden supports and covered them in paint in Bed, *a 1955 work that highly influenced Pop Art.*

tomer's personal needs or tastes. One woman had an elaborate French eighteenth-century canopy bed shortened so that it would fit into the submarine where she lives. Often, very tall or large individuals require larger beds with added reinforcements. Small beds have also been made. One of the most spectacular custom-made beds was a canopy bed presented by the showman P. T. Barnum to "General Tom Thumb" (Charles Sherwood Stratton) after his marriage in 1863 to Lavinia Warren. Thirty-six inches high and forty-eight inches long, the carved rosewood bed was a perfect fit for the

Above: This raised wooden bed and sleeping mat offer only a narrow escape from the noonday sun in Senegal, West Africa.

Opposite: A mosquito net hangs over the Medigayi family's bed in Djajibinni, Mauritania. The room was painted fifteen years ago by a relative, Fenda Gandega.

Overleaf: A sleeping bag and tent form an outdoor bed and bedroom on Roan Mountain in Tennessee.

179

Above: Artist Gerd Verschoor designed a bedroom for his friend Rob Houtenbos, whose surname means "bundles of wood." In honor of Rob's family name, Gerd created a headboard composed of individual bundles of wood. Each bundle represents a member of the Houtenbos family.

Left: Architect Brian Murphy designed this minimalist bedroom in Venice, California, for photographer Philip Dixon. The tatami mat rests within a raised cement curb.

Opposite: Fashioned after a patchwork quilt, these flowers have been made into a bed cover by artist Gerd Verschoor. The headboard is a fence that surrounds and protects a fictitious sleeper as it would a garden.

Above: This bed, designed by Marie-Paule Pellé, was hand made by a blacksmith. It was designed to resemble a gondola, floating in the middle of the room. With its high curved ends that look like wings, this is perhaps more accurately a bed of flight— an appropriate metaphor for its occupant, a woman who travels all over the world.

Opposite: Thought to have belonged to the Marquise de la Païva, a famous courtesan of the nineteenth century, this unusual carved walnut bed is adorned with sculpted cupids and a representation of Leda and the Swan.

Overleaf: This cave-hut is a reconstruction of one of the most primitive types of buildings in nineteenth-century Flanders. This one was inhabited by a broommaker who made his brooms in the room next door. The bed is a simple structure whose mattress is made of the same straw used to make the brooms.

three-foot groom and his two-foot-eight-inch bride. The bed is displayed today at the Barnum Museum in Bridgeport, Connecticut, along with an even smaller brass bed used by Tom Thumb when he was seven years old and twenty-five inches tall.

There are also people who prefer to sleep on exotically shaped beds; round, heart-shaped, and square beds are common variations. For many years Hugh Hefner slept on a round bed. Mae West liked to recline on an elaborate gilded bed shaped like a swan. Heart-shaped beds can be found in honeymoon suites in Las Vegas and the Poconos.

From as far back as ancient Egypt, miniature beds have been designed for dolls. Fine dollhouse furniture usually was fashioned to match the popular styles of the era. At the turn of the century, for example, oak beds were in great demand in both Europe and the United States. Doll's beds of that time were also fashioned from oak or imitation oak—either a light-colored wood resembling oak or a soft wood grained to look like oak. Often these tiny beds were fitted as well with hand-stitched dollsize bedcoverings.

184

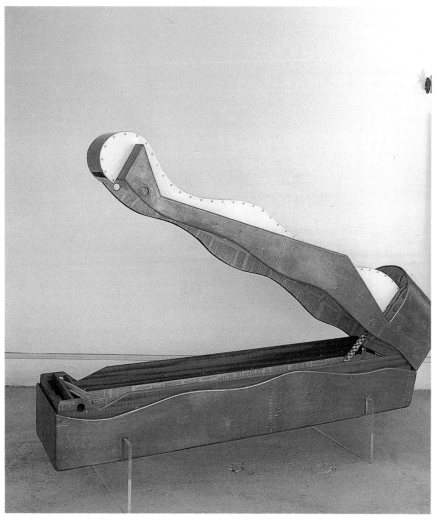

Pets, too, have enjoyed custom-made beds. In eighteenth-century France, for example, dogs and monkeys—the popular pets of the day—slept in small, elaborately designed models of their owners' beds. In contemporary Normandy, a woman has an enormous collection of antique beds; many of them are dog beds used by her large family of dogs. The beds are complete with canopies and bedspreads.

In today's world, where the desire to understand the universe has led to its exploration, astronauts have experienced sleeping in extraterrestrial environments. The NASA bed is perhaps a glimpse of a future in which colonies of people from earth will visit other worlds with different gravities. The most striking characteristic of the NASA bed is its sleep restraints, designed to keep the astronauts from floating away when sleeping in weightless atmospheres. Due to the lack of gravity in space, an astronaut may sleep in any position—upside down, horizontal, or vertical.

Left: While traveling in Egypt, artist and designer Pucci de Rossi was impressed by the sarcophagi he saw there. He appreciated not only their imposing beauty but also their meaning: Materially, they represent the idea of the beyond. By calling this work "From Here to Eternity," the artist humorously conceived a piece of furniture that one could use during one's lifetime as a daybed, and after death for the final trip.

Opposite: A fitting, though unusual, symbol for eternal rest, this bed tombstone, photographed by Lilo Raymond, marks a grave in a placid New England cemetery.

Overleaf: A forest floor covered with moss often looks soft and inviting. Artist Gerd Verschoor embraces this concept by building an actual bed of moss in the forest in Kaastert, Belgium.

189

FOUNDATIONS

The bed is the most important piece of furniture in the home. In it we spend a third of our lives, resting, sleeping, loving, convalescing. A good bed enables us to sleep soundly, encouraging our physical and emotional well-being.

The earliest bed was a sack, stuffed nightly with soft material. The stuffing varied according to the sleeper's means and preferences—it could be anything from straw to horsehair to wool to down. As medicine and technology advanced, the hygiene of beds increasingly became a concern. The inventions of the metal spring during the Industrial Revolution and foam during the 1940s were vital to the development of the innerspring mattress commonly used today. Modern mattresses are easy to care for, permanently shaped, and hygienic as well.

Today's bed most commonly consists of an innerspring mattress

197

Page 192: This gilded iron bed dates from 1865. A cameo adorns the headboard.

Page 193: Made of cast iron and brass, this turn-of-the-century American bed comes from Pamela Scurry's Wicker Garden.

Pages 194 and 195: A seventeenth-century gilt bed inhabits a vast bedroom of Balthus's castle in Montecalvello, Italy.

Page 196: Early mattresses were stuffed with a variety of materials. Here, one made of straw lies beneath another made of feathers.

Page 197: An unusual blue-green French-style bed was made in California in the 1920s.

Above, left: Dorothea Lange recorded a struggling mother in the 1930s loading her possessions, including mattresses, onto a truck.

Above, right: Mattresses used to be aired outdoors. This one sits in a window in Paris.

Opposite: The term "making a bed" comes from the days when people filled bags of fabric with straw or other soft material.

Overleaf: An innerspring mattress and down pillows are the basics of a contemporary bed.

and a box spring, which provides the mattress with needed support. These "sleep sets" can rest on the floor, a metal frame, or a more elaborate bedstead. Traditionally, a bedstead has a headboard and footboard, joined together by a frame and supported on four legs. There are numerous variations, from platform beds to those with exotic shapes. Bedsteads usually are constructed from wood or metal, in a choice of styles—from antique to contemporary—to suit any taste. The price of the bedstead generally is determined by the materials used, the workmanship, and the style of the piece.

Beds come in many shapes and sizes. Standardized mattress sizes are a relatively recent development—king, queen, full, double, and twin sizes were American developments in the 1950s. A bed should be about six inches longer than its occupant and should allow for freedom of movement from side to side. The standard American bed sizes are as follows: twin: 39" × 75"; full/double: 54" × 75"; queen: 60" × 80"; king: 76" × 80"; California king: 72" × 84".

The ideal mattress cradles the back so that the spine maintains the same position it has when the person is standing. Comfort and support are strictly a personal matter—one manufacturer's "firm" mattress may feel harder than another's "extra firm." If the mattress is too hard or too soft, the body's muscles will work constantly to straighten the spine and can lead to morning backache or headache.

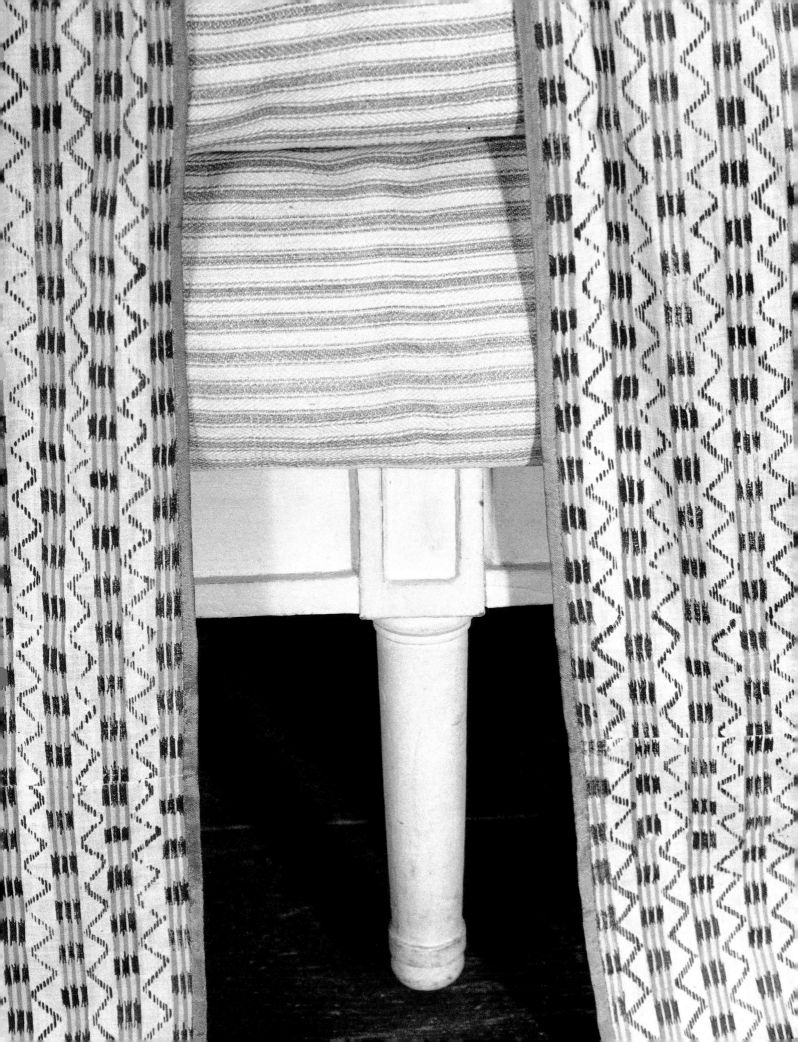

A new mattress can (and should) be checked for squeaks and buoyancy simply by sitting and lying on it. Examine as well the support for the area where the body's weight is concentrated (i.e., the middle). A mattress should be particularly supportive to the heaviest parts of the body. If a new bed is going to be shared, it should be chosen by both partners, especially if their body sizes and weights are notably different.

The quality of the inner construction of a mattress and box spring determines how long a bed will last. For best performance, there should be more than 300 coils in a full-size innerspring, more than 375 in a queen, and more than 450 in a king. There should be several layers

Top, left: Rope is latticed through this bed frame, allowing the bed to be adjusted for a good night's sleep. The bed is "tightened" by turning the ropes with a key, hence the origin of the term "sleep tight."

Top, right: This folding bed in the Skogaholm Manor at Skansen, in Stockholm, belonged to a baroness. The footboard could be adjusted to make the bed shorter during the day, thereby creating more space in the room. The bed is painted in a reddish brown hue to imitate mahogany.

Bottom: These African headrests were used by the Turkana people in Kenya for sleeping and relieving headaches. Headrests were also used by other tribes to keep intact elaborate hairstyles set with mud, clay, and natural pigments.

Opposite: Straw mattresses covered in blue ticking are piled high on a valet's bed at the Haga Pavilion in Stockholm.

Overleaf: Robert Homa, a designer and antique dealer, sleeps on cotton-filled futons and traditional Japanese woven straw mats. During the day, the futons are folded and stored behind an antique Japanese screen. All of the linens on the bed are made by members of Homa's family.

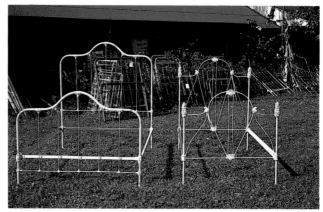

of quality upholstery materials—foam, fiberfill, cotton, and other natural fibers—to cushion the body. Keep in mind that the highest quality sleep sets are also the most expensive. For best results, both mattress and box spring should be replaced every eight to ten years.

Other types of mattresses include foam mattresses, futons, feather beds, water beds, and portable beds. A foam mattress is often a good and affordable alternative to an innerspring mattress. Some are made with a hard core, while others are a combination of different types of foam laminated together. Foam should have a minimum density of 2.0 pounds per cubic foot. The higher the number, the better the foam. The highest performance foams are the more traditional latex and the newer high-resilience polyurethanes.

A futon is another good alternative to a traditional mattress. Primarily made of layers of cotton, futons may also contain wool, foam, and horsehair. The different materials provide a range of texture and support: all-cotton futons are the softest, while those with a layer of horsehair in the center are the most firm. Some futons can be folded into couches or chairs, making them a practical and convenient addition to a small living area.

Above: Mass-produced from cast iron and steel, these late Victorian beds became popular in the 1880s because they were inexpensive and did not attract vermin as wooden beds did. After the start of World War I, the production of these beds in the United States was halted because the country needed iron to continue the war abroad. Beds of this kind often can be purchased inexpensively. Although many of them are rusted, parts are sometimes interchangeable and can be reused. Larger beds can be constructed by piecing together sections of other beds.

Opposite: Simple yet elegant, two Cooperstown pencil-post beds (one original, one copied) stand in this guest room. Ira Howard Levy designed the Shaker-style interior for his Connecticut retreat, Deer Run.

A feather bed is a soft cushion, usually the size of a mattress, filled with down and feathers. It provides the sleeper with extra cushioning and comfort. It can be placed under the bottom sheet or it can be encased in a feather bed cover and lie on top of the sleeper.

The modern water bed was designed in 1967 by a student from California. The concept, however, goes back three thousand years, when Persian nomads slept on goat skins filled with water. In the nineteenth century, water beds were used in hospitals to alleviate bedsores. Today's water beds are available in two styles: the "hardside" type is a vinyl mattress, with a liner and heater contained in a rigid frame; the newer "softside" style resembles a mattress/box spring combination. Both types offer a range of sensation, from "waveless" to "full motion." The vinyl should be a minimum of 20 mils thick.

Portable beds, including inflatable and roll-up mattresses, sleeping bags, canvas beds, and hammocks, provide a simple solution for accommodating occasional overnight guests, especially children. Inflatable mattresses require little storage space and are easily inflated with a pump. Roll-up mattresses are made from lightweight foam rubber and can be rolled or folded when not in use. Sleeping bags, still the most favored type of extra bedding, can be used alone or with an inflatable or roll-up mattress. Canvas beds, used by many armies around the world, have a steel frame and suspension strips that hold a canvas sleeping surface. They can be used with or without a portable mattress. Hammocks are usually made of netting or

Above, left: Two birds frame the head of a man in this nineteenth-century Neapolitan letto di matrimonio, *or marriage bed, made of handwrought iron.*

Above, middle: Delicate bows and tassels adorn this handcrafted and gilded Louis XVI marriage bed.

Above, right: A sleekly designed bed by Garouste and Bonetti recalls a budding tree.

Opposite: This antique panel dates from the eighteenth century. Its hand-carved goddess of fertility suggests that it may have been part of a bridal bed.

208

Left, top: An eighteenth-century bed painted with a Spanish pastoral scene is the focal element in the design and furnishings of this modern bedroom designed by Mariette Himes Gomez.

Left, bottom: This eighteenth-century Catalonian headboard from Betty Jane Bart Antiques was cut out of a flat piece of wood. Most likely part of a marriage bed, the headboard is painted with flowers and a medallion with a cupid in the center.

Opposite: Designer Jessica McClintock bleached this eighteenth-century bed, which is garlanded with carved roses and leaves.

211

canvas and hang suspended from two fixed points. They gently cradle the body and are comfortable and relaxing; however, they tend to be used more often for resting and napping than sleeping through the night.

Pillows

The choice of a pillow is a matter of comfort, support, and aesthetics. The way a pillow feels is determined by its degree of firmness and its contents. The filling materials include down, feathers, polyester fibers, and foam. Each type is available in soft, medium, and firm.

The standard pillow measures $20" \times 26"$. This is the most popular size and can be easily used on any size or type of bed. A queen-size pillow measures $26" \times 30"$ and a king-size $26" \times 36"$. They are intended for queen- or king-size beds, but, like the standard pillow, can be used on any size bed, depending on the needs and tastes of the sleeper. A European square is primarily French and measures $26" \times 26"$. A neck roll, as its name implies, is shaped like a roll. It measures $16" \times 5"$. A boudoir or baby pillow measures $12" \times 16"$ and can be used on a baby's bed or to accent a daybed or regular bed.

Above, left: An eighteenth-century English folding wing chair from Old World Weavers doubles for use with overnight guests. The back and arms drop down and removable legs can be screwed into the bottom of the slatted extension to lengthen the chair into a bed.

Above, right: A Gustavian-style guest room at the Skogaholm Manor House at Skansen, in Stockholm, is furnished with a collapsible steel traveling bed. The room is covered in painted linen wall coverings dating from 1793.

Opposite: A custom-made guest bed at the Zorn House in Dalarna, Sweden, doubles as a couch.

Overleaf: This French Empire bed with neo-Gothic toile de Jouy is in photographer François Halard's Manhattan home. An eclectic collection of fabrics and furnishings adds grace and beauty to this bedroom.

213

COVERINGS

Bed coverings—sheets, pillowcases, blankets, bedspreads, quilts, and duvets—have offered centuries of sleepers a good nights' sleep. These coverings many times have personal significance as well. Beautiful hand-made bed linens are often considered family heirlooms and passed down through the generations. They reflect the identity of our ancestors—the sisterhood that made, sold, and cared for linen sheets.

The bridal trousseau has been a tradition in many corners of the world. In the past, most marriages were arranged. A girl's wedding was planned moments after her birth, and soon thereafter the women in the family would start to prepare her trousseau. The making of these bed linens, towels, blankets, and pillowcases would consume entire lifetimes of women in families, villages, and convents.

Linens have always been expensive. In eighteenth-century

221

Page 216: A detail emphasizes the magnificence of the Empress's gilded bed at Château de Compiègne.

Page 217: From Porthault are crisp white linens elegantly laced with a satin bow and a yellow quilted eiderdown.

Pages 218 and 219: Curtains of heavy silk muslin and silk chiffon embroidered with gold thread form part of the impressive canopy of the empress's bed at Château de Compiègne.

Page 220: Dried hydrangeas hang alongside antique quilts at the country house of Raymond Waites.

Page 221: A farm bed at Skansen, in Stockholm, is covered with colorful woven bed covers.

Right: Watercolor drawings by Pamela Kogen show just a sampling of the many varied and elaborate canopies and coverings that were popular in France during the seventeenth and eighteenth centuries.

Opposite: The hangings on this Gustavian bed in the Skogaholm Manor House at Skansen, in Stockholm, are made of thin white cloth. The chair is signed by Stockholm cabinetmaker Erik Ohrmark.

France, the trousseau of a poor girl would consist of one sheet and one pillow, while a rich girl would have twelve sets of twelve. Not surprisingly, the less fortunate were often without any linens. Some people slept on burlap, while others would flatten, piece, and sew together fragments of linen undergarments gathered from scraps of material discarded by the rich.

The bed sheet has played an interesting role in the matrimonial conventions of some parts of the world. In small villages in Greece newlyweds have been known to hang out their sheets to air the morning after their wedding—the bloodstain proving the bride's virtue.

Sheets are available in a broad range of fabrics. The quality of the fabric is determined by the number of threads woven per inch—the higher the thread count, the better the material. A thread count of 300 or 350 will produce a very soft, beautiful sheet, as well as one that is strong and durable. The highest quality—and most expensive—sheets are made of linen. Spun from flax, linen has a cooling effect and is best suited for use in summertime or in hot climates. Linen sheets are a long-term investment; two sets of fine linen sheets can easily last twenty years.

Silk sheets are also durable but expensive. Warm in winter, they are luxurious to the eye and touch.

Cotton is the most popular fiber for bed sheets, used either alone or in combination with linen, silk, or polyester. Cotton sheets are absorbent, making them practical for any climate, and long-lasting, becoming more comfortable with age. Cotton flannel sheets are also available; these have a napped surface on both sides, providing extra warmth, comfort, and softness.

The size of the sheet is determined by the size of the bed. A bed is usually made with two sheets: a fitted, or bottom, sheet that conforms to the contour of the mattress; and a flat, or top, sheet, that lies on top of the fitted sheet and under the bed cover. Bottom sheets are sometimes oversized to accommodate extra-thick mattresses and/or feather beds, foam, or mattress pads.

Coverings for the pillow include pillow protectors, pillowcases, and shams. A pillow is first placed in a pillow protector—a zippered

Above, left: A luxuriously draped French Empire bed with a mahogany crown is still in use at a nineteenth-century château in Meursault, France.

Above, right: Printed linen hangings surround the headboard of a folding bed in the Skogaholm Manor House. The print is based on an original fabric found in a palace in Stockholm.

Opposite: The curtains of a valet's bed at the Haga Pavilion in Stockholm allow for complete privacy from the rest of the room.

pillowcase that protects the surface of the bare pillow, then slid into a pillowcase and/or a sham. A pillow sham differs from a pillowcase in that it is flanged or ruffled on the sides, and opens in the back, rather than on the side.

Bed coverings include blankets, blanket covers, bedspreads, quilts, and duvets. A good blanket combines warmth with lightness; it should be at least as wide as the bed. Wool blankets are the most popular, although cotton blankets make good summer coverings. The best wool blankets are those made of merino, cashmere, or long-pile mohair; other high-quality blankets include the traditional wool tartans of Scotland and Wales, woven Native American blankets, and embroidered woolen rugs. Avoid blankets made from synthetic fabrics—they tend to lose their fluffiness after one washing. In cold areas and in winter, today's electric blankets and mattress pads often are used in place of yesterday's heated bricks and hot-water bottles.

A blanket cover, which is usually a little heavier than a sheet, is used to protect and cover the blanket. During the summer, or in

Above: This Louis XVI bed, covered in blue-and-white Indian cotton, is part of Lillian Williams's collection of beds in Normandy. The walls in this room were hand painted.

Opposite: Barbara Tober's lit de glace, or mirrored bed, is draped in fine lace and dressed in an exquisite collection of both new and antique linens.

Overleaf: A collection of luxurious antique embroidered linens is the focus of this interior setting created by designer William Walter in the home of Tom Booth.

Above: In the master bedroom of a house designed by John Saladino is a collection of sumptuous pale linens and pillows.

Opposite: Textured pillows edged in black-and-white trim are always fluffed perfectly upright in Ian Schrager's Paramount Hotel in Manhattan.

warm climates, the blanket cover can be used in place of a blanket as a simple, lightweight bed covering for the top sheet.

A bedspread gives a finishing touch to a bed. It can be removed at night or turned back for sleeping. Bedspreads are usually made from heavy woven cottons, tapestry-like materials, candlewick, lace, or a crocheted or knitted fabric.

Originally a poor family's bedspread, the quilt today is admired as folk art, with antique quilts selling for thousands of dollars. When the first settlers left Europe for America, they took with them their three-layer coverlets. With the shortage of fabric in the early years in the new country, the women patched these coverlets as they wore out. By the eighteenth century, quilting had become a tradition among pioneer women. Quilts are composed of three layers—a top, a batting or lining, and a backing—and are usually made of cotton or wool.

A duvet is a down- or feather-filled comforter widely used in Scandinavia and mid-European countries, and increasingly popular in North America. Ideally, a duvet should be at least eighteen inches

HEMINGWAY
ROOSEVELT
GARY Co
CHEVAL
L. de VIL
CH. CHAPLIN
Présidence Etats-Unis.

Above, left: At D. Porthault & Co., each set of linens is an original work of art. Before they are transferred to the sheets, designs are created and refined on paper.

Above, right: A guest room at the Porthaults' house in Emance, France, has a bed draped and covered in a print called "Les Bouches."

Left: "Les Bleus Roses," a print from the 1930s, adorns this Porthault guest room in Emance, France.

Opposite: An assortment of folders from the archives of D. Porthault & Co. reveals only a fraction of Porthault's illustrious clientele.

Overleaf: Bette Midler's bedroom has a bed inspired by Charles Rennie Mackintosh. The bed is covered by one of the quilts from Midler's extensive collection.

233

wider than the bed. It provides comfortable, self-adjusting warmth, is very lightweight, and gives off almost no dust. Because of its insulating properties, no other blankets are needed, and bed-making becomes an easy task. The highest quality of natural filling in the duvet is either white goose down or duck down. Less expensive fillings are labeled "down and feathers," meaning more down than feathers, or "feathers and down," meaning more feathers than down. The greater the amount of down clusters, the warmer the duvet. Duvets should be aired occasionally and specially dry-cleaned if necessary. Synthetic fillings are also available; these have the advantage of being nonallergenic and easily washable.

Duvet covers are essential to protect the duvet. Usually made from sheetlike fabric, these covers button, snap, or fold closed. They are easily washable and allow for a duvet to be used as an alternative to a top sheet or bedspread.

Other commonly used bed coverings include mattress pads and mattress covers, which protect both mattress and box spring and are available in quilted cotton, wool, fleece, and convoluted foam; and bed skirts or dust ruffles, decorative mattress covers that usually hang down over three sides of a bed in a fourteen-inch drop.

Caring for, storing, and washing antique linens

Linens from the turn of the century are often stained from rust, oxidation, food, or liquids. If the linen is of museum quality, it should be given to a professional to clean. Most antique linens, however, can withstand gentle laundering.

To treat spots, place the linen in hot water and let it soak until the water is cold. If the linen is still not clean, repeat the process. If spots continue to remain, apply a very mild detergent to them and then hand-wash the linen with a mild soap. Do not use chlorine bleach. Never rub or scrub the linen; the motion of the water should be sufficient for cleansing. The linen can be machine-dried for a few minutes to remove excess moisture and wrinkles; then it should be hung on a line to dry.

The best time to begin ironing is when the linen is still damp. Place the embroidered side on an ironing board that is covered with terry cloth so as not to crush the work. Always press with the grain to maintain the shape. Gently flatten the fabric when ironing; never

Patchwork quilts can be obtained from a number of different sources, among them antique dealers and flea markets. These special coverings can be used on bedroom walls, chairs, tables, and, of course, beds. Often the handiwork of several people, these quilts possess a unique spirit and heritage.

Right, top: A collection of antique bed linens and bed covers is carefully stored in the loft of the linen collector and manufacturer Patrizia Anichini. The linens are best stored on special hangers that allow air to circulate among the linens when they are not being used.

Right, bottom: This linen closet belongs to Jan Dutton, the owner and designer of a linen company called Paper White. One of her greatest pleasures is to style a bed much as a painter approaches a painting: From her enormous collection of sheets and coverings she chooses the colors and textures with which to make her bed.

Opposite: Antique pieces from Madeleine Porthault's collection of linens include bed sets of pink crepe de Chine embroidered with Richelieu lace, linen hand-embroidered with "beauvais stitch," and linen faced with beige Venetian lace.

238

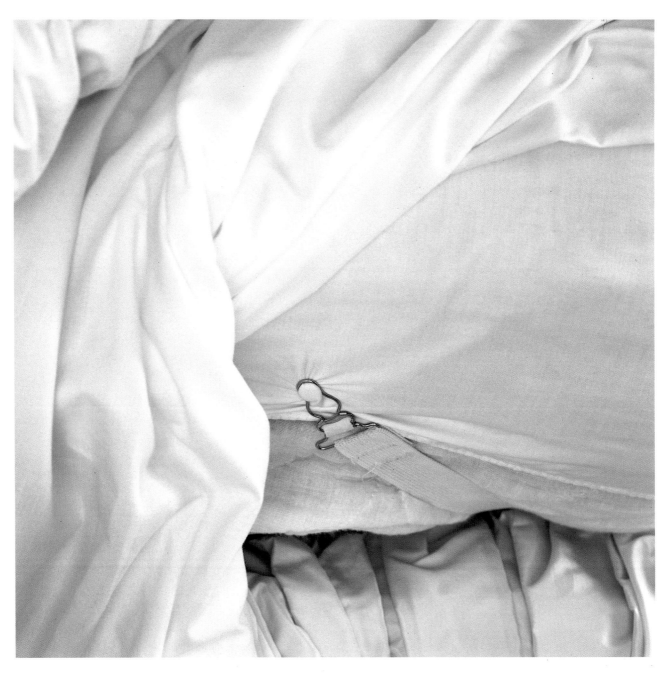

Above: Sheet suspenders, elastic straps that fasten to the bottom sheet and slide under the mattress, keep the sheet taut and snug around the mattress.

Opposite: A down pillow and a bag full of linens wait to be aired and laundered.

Overleaf: Nothing is better than the sweetness obtained by hanging linens out on a line to dry in the sun and fresh air.

pull the linen. Consider only ironing the "cuff" that will show; if the linen is placed at the bottom of other sheets or towels in the linen closet, their weight will naturally press out remaining wrinkles.

For short-term storage, linens may be washed, folded, and used like any other bed covering. Long-term storage is more involved. The linens should be covered in acid-free paper and stored in a box lined with unbleached muslin. Linens that are stored and rarely used should be washed and air-dried once or twice a year so that mold will not form on the creases.

240

SOURCES

BEDS AND LINENS

ABC CARPET & HOME
888 Broadway
New York, NY 10003 / (212) 473-3000
(antique French, American, Italian, and Scandinavian beds, cradles, and bassinets; wide selection of contemporary linens and accessories)

ALICE'S ANTIQUES
505 Columbus Avenue
New York, NY 10024 / (212) 874-3400
(continental and art deco beds and linens)

CONRAN'S HABITAT
160 East 54th Street
New York, NY 10022 / (212) 371-2225
Stores also located elsewhere in New York, in Connecticut, Massachusetts, New Jersey, Pennsylvania, Washington, DC, Bethesda, and Los Angeles.
(contemporary and traditional beds, linens, comforters, and pillows)

CRATE & BARREL
646 North Michigan Avenue
Chicago, IL 60611 / (312) 787-5900
Stores also located in Boston, Washington, DC, Minnesota, Texas, and California.
(contemporary metal, Shaker-, and mission-style beds; contemporary linens)

FLORENCE DE DAMPIERRE
79 Greene Street
New York, NY 10012 / (212) 966-5474
(beds and fine linens from Europe and the United States)

Page 244: An eighteenth-century hand-carved Venetian wedding bed has been partially restored for the collection of Iris Barrel Apfel. The headboard bears its original painting of a carnival scene.

Page 245: A star of gold leaf hangs above a daybed designed by Feldman–Hagan and Howard Christian.

Pages 246 and 247: This black-and-white photograph of a summer bed in Amagansett was taken by Lilo Raymond in 1977.

FORTUNOFF
1300 Old Country Road
Westbury, New York 11590 / (516) 832-9000
Stores also located in New Jersey.
(brass, wood, and steel beds; wide selection of contemporary and traditional linens, comforters, pillows, and accessories)

IKEA
1000 Center Street
Elizabeth, NJ 07202 / (201) 289-4488
Stores also located in Pennsylvania, New York, Maryland, Washington, DC, and California.
(Swedish-style metal and wood beds, cribs, and cradles; wide selection of linens)

MATTAWAN
491 Broadway
New York, NY 10012 / (212) 226-5825
(contemporary Shaker- and mission-style beds; natural-fiber linens, blankets, comforters, and pillows)

PIERRE DEUX
870 Madison Avenue
New York, NY 10021 / (212) 570-9343
Stores also located in Atlanta, Boston, Houston, Kansas City, Palm Beach, Philadelphia, Toronto, Washington, DC, Winnetka, and California.
(steel canopy and sleigh beds; French country linens)

BEDS

ACROPOLIS
2510 Main Street
Santa Monica, CA 90405 / (213) 396-7611
(contemporary and modern beds)

ALBEE
715 Amsterdam Avenue
New York, NY 10025 / (212) 662-5740
(cribs, bassinets, and accessories)

ARISE FUTONS
57 Greene Street
New York, NY 10012 / (212) 925-0310
Stores also located elsewhere in New York, in Chicago, and Florida.
(futons, mattresses, and bed frames)

AT HOME FURNISHINGS
3811 Porter Street NW
Washington, DC 20016 / (202) 537-1234
(futons and sofa beds)

BABY PALACE
181 Seventh Avenue
New York, NY 10011 / (212) 924-3700
(cribs, bassinets, cradles, and juvenile beds)

BEAU SEJOUR ANTIQUES
8817 Beverly Boulevard
Los Angeles, CA 90048 / (213) 271-1279
(reproduction and French eighteenth-century antique beds)

BELLINI
1305 Second Avenue
New York, NY 10021 / (212) 517-9233
(Italian furniture for infants)

BRIAN RUSSELL DESIGNS
2537 Broad Avenue
Memphis, TN 38112 / (901) 327-1210
(forged iron and wood custom-made beds)

THE CHILDREN'S ROOM
318 East 45th Street
New York, NY 10017 / (212) 687-3868
(Scandinavian and American juvenile beds)

COBWEB ANTIQUE IMPORTS
116 West Houston Street
New York, NY 10012 / (212) 505-1558
(nineteenth-century Spanish and Portuguese beds)

COUNTRY STORE
P.O. Box 17696
Whitefish Bay, WI 53217 / (414) 263-1919
(willow beds and furniture)

CURRENT
1201 Western Avenue, Suite 100
Seattle, WA 98101 / (206) 622-2433
(wood, metal, and upholstered modern beds)

DANIEL MACK
3280 Broadway
New York, NY 10017 / (212) 926-3880
(custom-made rustic and twig beds)

DELORENZO
958 Madison Avenue
New York, NY 10021 / (212) 249-7575
(contemporary and art deco beds and furniture)

DOOR STORE
One Park Avenue
New York, NY 10016 / (212) 679-9700
Stores also located elsewhere in New York, and in New Jersey.
(contemporary and country beds)

EAST & ORIENT CO.
2901 North Henderson Avenue
Dallas, TX 75206 / (214) 826-1191
(European antique beds)

ESPACE LOGGIA
118 Spring Street
New York, NY 10012 / (212) 925-2836
(modular loft and pine beds, futons, convertible sofa beds, and daybeds)

EVERGREEN ANTIQUES
1249 Third Avenue
New York, NY 10021 / (212) 344-5664
(Swedish country pine beds)

FREDERICK P. VICTORIA & SON
154 East 55th Street
New York, NY 10022 / (212) 755-2549
*(custom-made, authentic reproductions of
antique beds)*

FUN FURNITURE
8451 Beverly Boulevard
Los Angeles, CA 90048 / (213) 655-2711
*(custom-made Formica and painted juvenile beds
and furniture)*

FURNITURE OF THE 20TH CENTURY
227 West 17th Street
New York, NY 10011 / (212) 929-6023
(wide selection of modern and contemporary beds)

GOLDEN OLDIES
132–29 33rd Avenue
Flushing, NY 11354 / (718) 445-4400
(antique and reproduction beds)

GRIFFIS STUDIOS
30 Essex Street
Buffalo, NY 14213 / (716) 886-3616
(custom-made modern and iron beds and furniture)

HBS
301 Chartres Street
New Orleans, LA 70130 / (504) 524-0314
*(eighteenth- and nineteenth-century French beds
and antiques)*

HOB NAIL ANTIQUES
Route 22
Box 93A
Pawling, New York 12564 / (914) 855-1623
*(turn-of-the-century metal, iron, and
brass bedsteads)*

HOWARD KAPLAN
FRENCH COUNTRY STORE
35 East Tenth Street
New York, NY 10003 / (212) 674-1000
(antique and reproduction French beds)

HUDDLE FURNITURE
11159 Santa Monica Boulevard
West Los Angeles, CA 90025 / (213) 478-5986
(American juvenile furniture)

JEAN PAUL BEAUJARD
209 East 76th Street
New York, NY 10021 / (212) 249-3790
(French antique beds)

LEWIS OF LONDON
215 East 51st Street
New York, NY 10022 / (212) 688-3669
(Italian cribs, cradles, and juvenile beds)

LYMAN DRAKE
2901 South Harbor Boulevard
Santa Ana, CA 92704 / (714) 979-2811
(European beds)

MARIO VILLA
3908 Magazine Street
New Orleans, LA 70115 / (504) 895-8731
(contemporary neoclassical-style beds)

MICHAEL SHANNON ASSOCIATES
1888 Illinois Street, Department M
San Francisco, CA 94124 / (415) 641-9444
(metal and canopy beds)

MODERN AGE
795 Broadway
New York, NY 10003 / (212) 674-5603
(contemporary furniture and accessories)

MODERNE
111 North Third Street
Philadelphia, PA 19106 / (215) 923-8536
(art deco beds)

MOSSA
1214 Washington Avenue
St. Louis, MO 63103 / (314) 241-5199
(modern Italian and French beds and furniture)

NEWEL ART GALLERIES
425 East 53rd Street
New York, NY 10022 / (212) 758-1970
*(renaissance through art deco beds, furnishings,
and accessories)*

NIALL SMITH ANTIQUES
AND DECORATIONS
344 Bleecker Street
New York, NY 10014 / (212) 255-0664
(neoclassical beds)

NORTHWEST FUTON CO.
400 SW 2nd Avenue
Portland, OR 97204 / (503) 242-0057
(futons and frames)

PAMELA SCURRY'S WICKER GARDEN
1318 Madison Avenue
New York, NY 10128 / (212) 410-7000
(antique wicker beds)

PIERRE DEUX ANTIQUES
369 Bleecker Street
New York, NY 10014 / (212) 243-7740
*(eighteenth- and nineteenth-century French
country beds)*

PINE COUNTRY ANTIQUES
71 Mercer Street
New York, NY 10012 / (212) 674-9663
(pine beds)

SCHNEIDER'S
20 Avenue A
New York, NY 10009 / (212) 228-3540
(infant and juvenile furniture and beds)

WICKER GARDEN'S BABY
1327 Madison Avenue
New York, NY 10128 / (212) 410-7001
(infant wicker and iron beds)

WORKBENCH
470 Park Avenue South
New York, NY 10016 / (212) 532-7900
Stores also located elsewhere in New York,
in New Jersey, Connecticut, Boston,
and Philadelphia.
(juvenile and adult beds)

LINENS

AD HOC SOFTWARES
410 West Broadway
New York, NY 10012 / (212) 925-2652
(contemporary linens)

AMERICA HURRAH
766 Madison Avenue
New York, NY 10021 / (212) 535-1930
(antique quilts)

ANICHINI
745 Fifth Avenue, Suite 2007
New York, NY 10019 / (212) 752-2130
(fine Italian linens)

ANN LAWRENCE ANTIQUES
250 West 39th Street
New York, NY 10018 / (212) 302-6100
(large collection of antique linens)

AUREA
20 East 67th Street
New York, NY 10021 / (212) 650-0600
(fine Italian linens)

CRAFT CARAVAN
63 Greene Street
New York, NY 10012 / (212) 431-6669
(handwoven African fabrics and coverings)

D. PORTHAULT & CO.
18 East 69th Street
New York, NY 10021 / (212) 688-1661
(fine French linens)

DESCAMPS BOUTIQUE
454 Columbus Avenue
New York, NY 10024 / (212) 769-9260
Stores also located elsewhere in New York, in
Boston, Philadelphia, and Washington, DC.
(imported French linens)

E. BRAUN & CO.
717 Madison Avenue
New York, NY 10021 / (212) 838-0650
(European and American linens in cotton, linen, and silk)

FRETTE
799 Madison Avenue
New York, NY 10021 / (212) 988-5221
Store also located in Los Angeles.
(fine Italian linens)

JUDITH AND JAMES MILNE
506 East 74th Street
New York, NY 10021 / (212) 472-0107
(antique quilts)

LAURA FISHER ANTIQUES
1050 Second Avenue
New York, NY 10022 / (212) 243-5456
(American antique quilts and blankets)

LERON
750 Madison
New York, NY 10021 / (212) 249-3188
(fine European and American linens)

LINENS LIMITED
240 North Milwaukee Street
Milwaukee, WI 53202 / (800) 637-6334
(restoration and cleaning of fine and antique linens)

PAPER WHITE LTD.
P.O. Box 956
Fairfax, CA 94930 / (415) 457-7673
(fine white linen and lace bed linens)

PRATESI
829 Madison Avenue
New York, NY 10021 / (212) 288-2315
(fine Italian linens)

QUILTS OF AMERICA
431 East 73rd Street
New York, NY 10021 / (212) 535-1600
(antique quilts)

RALPH LAUREN
867 Madison Avenue
New York, NY 10021 / (212) 606-2100
Stores located across the United States.
(full collection of linens and accessories)

RENATE HALPERN GALLERIES
325 East 79th Street
New York, NY 10021 / (212) 988-9316
(nineteenth-century Chinese bed covers)

SARAJO
568 Broadway
New York, NY 10012 / (212) 966-6156
(handwoven textiles)

SCANDIA DOWN
200 Marketplace Tower
2025 First Avenue
Seattle, WA 98121 / (800) 848-3096
Stores located across the United States.
(full line of down products for the bed)

SHEET SUSPENDERS
P.O. Box 0355
Coral Gables, FL 33243-0355
(suspenders that help sheets fit tautly on mattress)

SHERIDAN
595 Madison Avenue
New York, NY 10022 / (800) 777-9563
Stores located across the United States.
(contemporary linens)

THOMAS K. WOODWARD
835 Madison Avenue
New York, NY 10021 / (212) 988-2906
(antique quilts)

TREADLES
95 Horatio Street
New York, NY 10014 / (212) 633-0072
By appointment only.
(handwoven baby and adult blankets)

TROUVAILLE FRANÇAISE
552 East 87th Street
New York, NY 10128 / (212) 737-6015
By appointment only.
(vintage and antique linens)

VICTORIAN GARDEN
136–58 72nd Avenue
Flushing, NY 11367 / (718) 544-1657
By appointment only.
(vintage and antique linens)

THERAPEUTIC BEDDING

BIO CLINIC CO.
4083 East Airport Drive
Ontario, CA 91761 / (714) 989-2534
(egg-crate foam mattress pads, anatomical pads, and other kinds of therapeutic bedding)

BETTER SLEEP COUNCIL
P.O. Box 13
Washington, DC 20044
(write for a guide on how to sleep better)

MAIL-ORDER BEDS AND LINENS

BOSTON & WINTHROP
35 Banks Terrace
Swampscott, MA 01907 / (617) 593-8248
(hand-painted beds for children)

BUNDLES
1456 Second Avenue, Suite 158
New York, NY 10021 / (800) 283-8900
(blankets, pillows, and quilts for babies)

CHAMBERS
Mail Order Department
P.O. Box 7841
San Francisco, CA 94120 / (800) 334-9790
(bed linens, blankets, and accessories)

COMANCHE DESIGN
3019½ Olympic Boulevard
Santa Monica, CA 90404
(800) 328-9592 (outside of 213 area code)
(213) 453-9592 (within 213 area code)
(log cabin–inspired beds)

THE COMPANY STORE
500 Company Store Road
LaCrosse, WI 54601-4477 / (800) 323-8000
(100% cotton bed linens, pillows, and comforters)

COUNTRY WORKSHOP
95 Rome Street
Newark, NJ 07105 / (800) 526-8001
(finished and unfinished storage, bunk, and trundle beds and headboards; platform beds on special order)

CRATE & BARREL
646 North Michigan Avenue
Chicago, IL 60611 / (312) 787-5900
(contemporary metal, Shaker-, and mission-style beds; contemporary linens)

CUDDLEDOWN OF MAINE
42 North Elm Street
P.O. Box 667
Yarmouth, ME 04096 / (207) 846-9781
(European down comforters and linens)

DAS FEDERBETT
961 Gapter Road
Boulder, CO 80303 / (303) 494-2343
(comforters, pillows, and feather beds)

DOMESTICATIONS
340 Poplar Street
Hanover, PA 17333-0040 / (717) 633-3333
(linens and accessories)

DOUGLAS ASSOCIATES
14 Duck Pond Road
Norwalk, CT 06855 / (800) 732-5661
(contemporary, iron, and four-poster beds)

EDDIE BAUER
P.O. Box 3700
Seattle, WA 98124 / (800) 426-8020
(sleeping bags, flannel sheets, blankets, down comforters, and country beds)

ELLENBURG'S WICKER & CASUAL
Stamey Farm Road
P.O. Box 5628
Statesville, NC 28677 / (704) 873-2900
(rattan and wicker casual beds)

ESPACE LOGGIA
118 Spring Street
New York, NY 10012 / (212) 925-2836
(modular loft and pine beds, futons, convertible sofa beds, and daybeds)

THE FAIRYLAND COLLECTION
P.O. Box 72640
Chattanooga, TN 37407 / (800) 544-7045
(hand-decorated wicker beds for children)

FEATHERED FRIENDS
2013 Fourth Avenue
Seattle, WA 98121 / (206) 441-8229
(sleeping bags, down pillows, and comforters)

GARNET HILL
262 Main Street
Franconia, NH 03580 / (800) 622-6216
(natural-fiber bed linens, blankets, comforters, and pillows)

HAMMACHER SCHLEMMER
9180 Le Saint Drive
Fairfield, OH 45014 / (800) 543-3366
(pillows, blankets, and sleep-sound generators)

HEAVENLY DOWN
419 Allan Court
Healdsburg, CA 95448 / (707) 431-1400
(down comforters and pillows, feather beds, and sleeping bags)

THE HORCHOW COLLECTION
P.O. Box 620048
Dallas, TX 75262-0048 / (800) 527-0303
(fine linens, blankets, and accessories; country and canopy beds)

JC PENNEY TELEMARKETING
One Lincoln Center, 14th Floor
P.O. Box 659000
Dallas, TX 75240 / (800) 222-6161
(mattresses, beds, and linens)

L. L. BEAN
Freeport, ME 04033 / (800) 221-4221
(sleeping bags, flannel sheets, blankets, hammocks, down comforters, and country beds)

LANDS' END
One Lands' End Lane
Dodgeville, WI 53595 / (800) 356-4444
(linens and accessories for children and adults)

PACIFIC COAST FEATHER CO.
1964 Fourth Avenue South
Seattle, WA 98134 / (206) 624-1057
(feather beds, down pillows, and comforters)

QUILTS UNLIMITED
440A Duke of Gloucester Street
Williamsburg, VA 23185 / (804) 253-8700
(antique and new quilts)

SHAKER WORKSHOP
P.O. Box 1028
Concord, MA 01742 / (617) 646-8985
(reproduction Shaker beds)

SIMPLY SOUTHERN
P.O. Box 376
Toccoa, GA 30577 / (404) 886-7454
(reproduction European beds)

VICTORIAN GARDEN
136–58 72nd Avenue
Flushing, NY 11367 / (718) 544-1657
(vintage and antique linens)

SHOWROOMS
Open to the trade only. Call for information.

AVERY BOARDMAN
979 Third Avenue
New York, NY 10022 / (212) 688-6611
(upholstered headboards; electric, high-rise, trundle, canopy, and sofa beds; horsehair mattresses)

BISCHOFF LACE
973 South Westlake Boulevard / Suite 208
Westlake Village, CA 91361 / (800) 331-5223
(fine imported linens)

CHARLES BECKLEY
306 East 61st Street
New York, NY 10021 / (212) 759-8450
(custom-upholstered headboards, daybeds, boxsprings, and mattresses)

DAN RIVER
111 West 40th Street
New York, NY 10018 / (212) 554-5500
(wide selection of traditional and contemporary bed linens)

DONGHIA
979 Third Avenue
New York, NY 10022 / (212) 935-3713
(upholstered daybeds)

DUX INTERIORS
305 East 63rd Street
New York, NY 10021 / (212) 752-3897
(Swedish beds)

FIELDCREST CANNON
1271 Avenue of the Americas
New York, NY 10036 / (212) 957-2500
(wide selection of traditional and contemporary bed linens)

ICF
305 East 63rd Street
New York, NY 10021 / (212) 750-0900
(reproduction Alvar Aalto beds)

ILANA GOOR
979 Third Avenue
New York, NY 10011 / (212) 686-6400
(contemporary iron beds)

PHYLLIS MORRIS
8772 Beverly Boulevard
Los Angeles, CA 90048 / (213) 655-6238
(custom-upholstered headboards; wood and iron beds in a variety of styles)

RALPH LAUREN HOME COLLECTION
1185 Avenue of the Americas
New York, NY 10036 / (212) 642-8700
By account only.
(traditional iron, wood, and wicker beds; traditional and contemporary bed linens)

REVMAN
1211 Avenue of the Americas
New York, NY 10036 / (212) 840-7780
(traditional and contemporary bed linens)

SCANDINAVIAN DESIGN
127 East 59th Street
New York, NY 10022 / (212) 755-6078
(Finnish beds and furniture for adults and infants)

THOMAS DEANGELIS
1115 Broadway
New York, NY 10010 / (212) 620-0191
(custom-upholstered headboards and daybeds)

WAMSUTTA
1285 Avenue of the Americas
New York, NY 10019 / (212) 903-2000
(wide selection of traditional and contemporary bed linens)

WESTPOINT J.P. STEVENS
1185 Avenue of the Americas
New York, NY 10036 / (212) 930-2000
(wide selection of traditional and contemporary bed linens)

ACKNOWLEDGMENTS

There are many people whom I would like to acknowledge for their support and enthusiasm. It is with my deepest gratitude that I say thank you to those whose involvement enriched this project: my great friend Robyn Glaser, Gerd Verschoor, Paul Siskin, Peroucho Valls, Geoff Howell, Howard Christian, William Walter, Bienne Burckhardt, Pamela Kogen, Marilyn Glass, Arthur Williams, Joe Staiano, Oberto Gili, William Waldron, François Halard, Tim Street-Porter, Margaret Courtney-Clarke, John Hall, Fritz von der Schulenberg, Pascal Chevallier, Alexandre Bailhache, Evelyn Hofer, Robert Benson, and Richard Davies.

Thanks to my assistants for their thorough dedication: Cara Sadownick, Caroline Jouve Le Got, and Amelia Dare. Debra Jason brings joy to my life and work; other friends include Stephen Rhindress, Stephen Donelian, George Ross, Lewis Bloom, Sheri Sussman, Donna Chance, Jeannel Astarita, Tom Panizzi, Tom McWilliam, and Millie Martini. Thanks also to Paule, Leonard, Antonin, Garance, Lolo, Sylvia, Apollo, and to Tout Pour le Ménage for their fine photo processing and help.

I am grateful to Marc and Françoise Porthault for their continued support and Fiona Donnelly for her research and inspiring words. Thanks to Elizabeth Stapen of the Swedish Information Service, Nancy Butler, Iris and Carl Apfel, Lillian Williams, Jessica McClintock, and to Patrizia Anichini for the linens used on the front jacket. Meaningful conversations with Erena Bramos inspired me, as did a number of books, including *The Philosophy of the Bed* by Mary Eden and Richard Carrington, *On Going to Bed* by Anthony Burgess, *Beds* by Reginald Reynolds, *The Bed* by Cecil and Margery Gray, *The Love and Teachings of the Kama Sutra* by Indra Sinha, *The Art of Love* by Ovid, and the many works by Joseph Campbell.

Special thanks to Condé Nast Publications; Alexander Liberman; all my friends at *Bride's* magazine; my agent, Malaga Baldi; Micaela Porta, Barbara Sturman, Kathy Rosenbloom, Leslie Stoker; Cornelia Guest; Julio Vega for his beautiful design; and my editor, Jennie McGregor Bernard, whose perception and judgment are the best.

The love and encouragement of my family is so important to me—thanks to Joane and Bernard Archer; my sister, Nola Beldegreen, and Stephen Klein; Ann and Morris Miller; and Juliana Harkavy. My special love and gratitude to my soul mate, Elliot Mayrock, for his generosity, love, and patience.

This book would not have been possible without a few very special people. Barbara Tober has always inspired me and made it possible for me to work on this book. My thanks to Lilo Raymond for her beautiful images and loving friendship. Thibault Jeanson, with his clear vision and dedication to the subject, successfully captured the soul and decoration of beds from all over the world. Finally, my deepest gratitude to Michael and Berta Harkavy for their devotion and involvement in this project. Their partnership, talent, love, and guidance helped make this book a reality.

253

INDEX

*Page 252: This bed by Marcion was used by
visiting royalty at the Château de Compiègne.
Napoleon made certain that the red, gold,
and blue color scheme used in his imperial
quarters was not repeated for others.*

The photographs appearing on the following pages are printed with permission: Pages 2, 8 (middle), 40–41, 43, 46–47, 52, 53, 55 (top left and right), 56–57, 58, 62 (top), 87 (bottom), 94–95, 108, 109, 155, 169, 174–175, 188, 192 (originally published in *Bride's*), 193, 200–201, 203 (bottom), 207, 210, 213 (left), 236, 238 (bottom photograph originally published in *Bride's*), 240, 241, 242–243, 246–247: copyright © Lilo Raymond. Pages 14–15: copyright © Galen Rowell/Peter Arnold, Inc. Pages 24–25: Alexandre Bailhache; courtesy of Giorgio Franchetti and Beatrice Monti, and *HG*, copyright © 1990 by the Condé Nast Publications Inc. Page 28: Artistic Director M. P. Pellé/Photo Pascal Chevallier Vogue Decoration and Deborah Webster. Page 44: Courtesy of Hal Bromm, New York. Page 45: copyright © John M. Hall Photographs; originally published in *HG*. Pages 82–83: Thibault Jeanson; courtesy of *HG*, copyright © 1988 by the Condé Nast Publications Inc. Page 85: copyright © Fritz von der Schulenberg; caravan courtesy of Mary Montagu. Pages 97, 137, 144 (right): copyright © William

Waldron; pages 97, 144 (right) originally published in *Bride's*. Pages 118–119, 149, 157: Thibault Jeanson; courtesy of *HG*, copyright © 1989 by the Condé Nast Publications Inc. Page 162 (top): copyright © Robert Benson. Page 168: Richard Davies; courtesy of *HG*, copyright © 1987 by the Condé Nast Publications Inc. Page 170: Oberto Gili; courtesy of *Bride's*, copyright © 1985 by the Condé Nast Publications Inc. Page 173: Courtesy of Modern Age Galleries, New York. Page 176: Richard J. Linke; courtesy of the Adirondack Museum. Page 177 (left): courtesy of NASA. Pages 178, 179: From *African Canvas*, photographs and text by Margaret Courtney-Clarke, Rizzoli. Pages 180–181: copyright © Clyde H. Smith/Peter Arnold, Inc. Page 183: copyright © Tim Street-Porter. Pages 194–195: copyright © Evelyn Hofer; originally published in *HG*. Page 198 (left): Dorothea Lange/Library of Congress (LC-USF34-16456-E). Page 198 (right): Edouard Boubat/Agence Photographique TOP. Page 206: Wolf Brackrock; courtesy of *Architektur & Wohnen*. Page 230: copyright ©

François Halard. Pages 234–235: Tim Street-Porter; courtesy of Bette Midler and Harold Kipper, and *HG*, copyright © 1988 by the Condé Nast Publications Inc.

The artwork appearing on the following pages is printed with permission. Page 17: *Death of Sardanapalus*, Delacroix, Louvre copyright © R.M.N. Page 18: *The Princess and the Pea*, Dulac, Robert Harding Picture Library/Rainbird/The Victoria and Albert Museum. Page 44: *The Cradle*, Morisot, Louvre copyright © R.M.N. Page 74 (top): *Madame Récamier*, David, Louvre copyright © R.M.N. Page 98: *The Bolt*, Fragonard, Louvre copyright © R.M.N. Page 130: *The Bed*, Toulouse-Lautrec, Art Resource (945 Q11). Page 156: *The Sick Woman*, Vallotton, Lausanne, Collection Vallotton, Giraudon/Art Resource, NY (LAC 90089) copyright © 1991 ARS, NY/SPADEM. Page 172: *Maharajah's Bed*, Christofle, G. M. Bowman & Associates Inc. Page 177: *Bed*, copyright © Robert Rauschenburg/VAGA New York 1991.

255

The text for this book was set in
Adobe Caslon and was composed with
QuarkXpress 3.0 on a Macintosh IIsi and
output on a Linotronic L300 at
The Sarabande Press, New York, New York.
The display type was set in Meridien.

The book was printed and bound by
Toppan Printing Company, Ltd.,
Tokyo, Japan.